12 M

PRODUCTIVITY
PLANNER
for SUCCESSFUL
WOMEN

DR JACQUELINE N SAMUELS

https://tinyurl.com/AuthorJNSamuelsUK

This Planner belongs to:

_____

INTRODUCTION

This 12-month planner was created to:

✓ Help you define your goals

✓ Keep you focused

✓ Effectively manage your time

✓ Make you more productive

Productivity is a measure of the amount of work done within a specific length of time. The more work you complete during this time, the more productive you are. Apply the following six tips to help you be more productive and make the most effective use of this planner.

SIX TIPS TO BE MORE PRODUCTIVE

1. Gain Control Over Your Time

To organize your day, week, and month efficiently so that you get a lot done, you need to know how to gain control over your time.

2. Set Goals and Priorities

Before you can even start deciding on how to spend your time, you need to set your goals and priorities for the period in question. It works well to plan on a yearly basis and then translate that into monthly goals, weekly goals, and then finally into daily tasks.

3. Start with Major Yearly Planning

First, brainstorm and record at least one to three key goals for your year for each area of your life.

4. Translate Goals and Priorities into Tasks

If you write your goals correctly, it is easy to translate them into actionable tasks. For example, when you write a goal, it should include specifics and results. For example, "My goal is to write an 80,000-word Young Adult Novel by December 31, 2022."

When you see that goal, you can come up with tasks that need to be done, such as plotting, character development, writing, editing, book design, and so forth. Start from the result you want.. Separate the projects into smaller tasks that can be scheduled consistently and sequentially until the end date.

5. Prioritize Tasks

Sometimes this is the hardest part of time management and learning to get things done each day, week, and month. The best way to create priorities is to make smart goals, write the goals down, translate the goals to tasks, and put them in order of importance based on your values, morals, and needs.

Gaining control over your time starts with accepting that time management is a myth because you cannot stop time or control time. All you have control of is how you react to the time you've been given to reach your life goals.

6. Knowing Your Goals for Each Area of Your Life

Let's talk more about setting goals for each area of your life. When you want to plan better for each month, week, and day the best way to accomplish this is to start with yearly planning and set one to three goals for each area of your life.

Get very specific so that you can easily measure your progress as well as organize the actions and tasks that you need to take to reach your goals efficiently.

THINK ABOUT THE LIFE YOU WANT

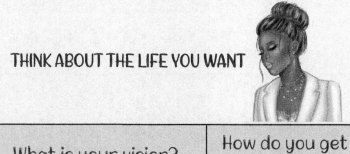

Date frame	What is your vision?	How do you get there?
6 months		
1 year		
1.5 year		
2 years		
3 years		
5 years		

THIS YEAR'S GOALS OVERVIEW

Year:

Personal goals	Health and Wellness goals

Business/ Work	Financial Goals

Spiritual goals	Other goals

Set annual goals for each area of your life - career, relationships, health, life...

You've probably heard of S.M.A.R.T goals before...and that's because it's a formula that works. Here's an overview:

SPECIFIC – Your goal needs to be spelled out very precisely and you also need to have a reason WHY behind your goal...some benefit or emotional attachment that will keep you focused. For example, a goal might be to earn $12,500 per month and onboard 5 new quality clients monthly in the next 90 days.

Using language that leaves no doubt as to what the goal is, why you want to achieve the goal, and how you will get there is very important. If you are not able to be detailed in your description of the goal, it will be hard to meet it. Take the time to do this part right.

MEASURABLE – If your goal cannot be quantified, then it's not a full goal and you won't know how when you have succeeded. An example of a measurable goal would be "I want to deposit to our bank account an additional 100 dollars per week. I'll accomplish this by writing five 500-word articles each week for a life coach."

ACTIONABLE / ACHIEVABLE – There are different things that "A" can stand for, but it's usually actionable or achievable. In order to achieve anything, you must take action. So, make your goal actionable, where you do something each day that will eventually result in an accomplished goal.

Goals should also be achievable, or you will quickly get frustrated. Be accurate about the time it takes to reach a goal, and what actions it takes to get there. Also, know who will be responsible for doing it.

REALISTIC / RELEVANT – "R" can stand for realistic or relevant, and both are important.. If you want your goal to succeed, it should most certainly be realistic, or you will fail. If you're currently making $500 a week and your goal is to increase that to $12,500 in 90 days, that's not realistic. However, you may be able to increase it by $300. Once you achieve that goal and are earning $800 a week, you can set a new goal to increase your income by another $500 a week or something similar.

Your goal should also be relevant to your life's vision and match your values. There's no point in making or achieving goals that have no relevance to your long-term life goals. You could instead use that time to reach goals that get you one step closer to actually reaching your life goals. So always ask yourself, if the goal is relevant to your life goals.

TIME BOUND / TIMELY / TRACKABLE – Various authors refer to the "T" in the S.M.A.R.T. acronym as time-bound, timely or trackable. All these t's are important parts of the goal creating and setting process. If you don't set a time limit and you can't track what is happening, your goal will be hard to quantify or show as achieved.

Deadlines are important, or your actions will take forever. The **Parkinson's Law** states that "Work expands to fill the time available for its completion.

If you have 24 hours to complete a project, the time pressure forces you to focus on execution, and you have no choice but to do only the bare essentials. If you are given two months, it can become a herculean task. The irony is that the end product of the shorter deadline may be almost inevitably of equal or higher quality due to greater focus.

S.M.A.R.T. GOALS

List The Required Information In The Apropriate Areas As Indicated

S SPECIFIC	What do you want to accomplish?

M MEASUBLE	How will you know you have accomplished your goal?

A ATTAINABLE.	How can the goal be accomplished?

R RELEVANT	Is the goal worth working hard to accomplish? Explain.

T TIMELY	By when will the goal be accomplished?

When it comes to time management, the 80/20 rule can be revolutionary. Sometimes known as the Pareto Principle, this rule helps to boost your productivity. Applying this rule allows you to prioritize your time and your tasks. It's vital at work and key to success. So, how does the principle work?

Out of any ten items, two are more valuable than the others put together. However, those two items are most likely to be the ones we delay and procrastinate on. The 80/20 rule ensures this doesn't happen.

How can you apply the rule in your own life? Write down 10 goals that you need to accomplish. Next, ask which of those goals is most important. Which one has the most positive impact? Which one is most essential? Which one is most time-pressured? Next, choose the next most vital goal. This identifies the "20" element of the equation. You now know which goals you need to work on first.

THE "EAT THE FROG" TECHNIQUE

The frog here is the most unpleasant task on the to-do list that you've drawn up. It's human nature to try to avoid unpleasant tasks. We're all guilty of putting off something that we must do but don't want to do.

When you avoid an unpleasant task, it's always on your mind. It stops you from getting on with other jobs that need to be done. It prevents you from focusing. You know all the time that the unpleasant task must be done. Why put it off? Do it first and get it out of the way!

THE 2-MINUTE RULE

The "2-minute rule" can make an enormous difference in your life. The concept is that if you've got a task that could be completed in 2 minutes, do it immediately. It's a time management strategy that dramatically improves your productivity. You'll eliminate procrastination and accomplish more every day.

TAKE A BREAK

It seems counterintuitive to take a break when there's work to be done. However, taking regular breaks helps to boost your memory, creativity and concentration.

If you work continuously for extended periods of time, you'll experience more stress. You'll also become more exhausted and won't be able to achieve your personal best. Taking frequent breaks helps to refuel and refresh your mind. This allows you to maximize your efficiency.

The "Do Later" list helps to keep your mind clear. You have a to-do list with all the immediate tasks you need to do. But, what do you do with the non-urgent tasks? Rather than keeping them in your head, note them down. This allows you to remain fully focused on the key tasks at hand. Yet, you won't forget about all those non-essential jobs that can be delayed until later.

While this type of list is a useful solution, it isn't foolproof. There's a danger that if a task ends up on the "Do Later" list, it just won't get done. Therefore, you should add a review date to each item. Note that review date in your planner.

The first step to overhauling your work approach is to identify the tasks you can ditch. Remember, eliminating isn't about being lazy. It's about staying efficient. It's about completing tasks that are essential rather than doing work purely for the sake of it.

It's easy to fall into the trap of thinking you're being productive if you're incredibly busy. Yet, this isn't necessarily true. You're only being productive if you're effective and efficient. It's possible to achieve a lot more by doing a lot less.

(NOT) TO-DO LISTS

"DO LATER" LIST	TASKS YOU CAN DITCH

If you look at all your tasks, there are probably many that you could delegate or outsource. Just because you can do everything yourself doesn't mean you should. Delegating and outsourcing can make you considerably more productive.

LISTS FOR OTHERS TO CHECK

TASKS YOU CAN DELEGATE	TO WHOM?

JANUARY

MONTH: _____

MONDAY	TUESDAY	WEDNESDAY	THURSDAY	FRIDAY	SATURDAY	SUNDAY
☐	☐	☐	☐	☐	☐	☐

MONDAY	TUESDAY	WEDNESDAY	THURSDAY	FRIDAY	SATURDAY	SUNDAY
☐	☐	☐	☐	☐	☐	☐

MONDAY	TUESDAY	WEDNESDAY	THURSDAY	FRIDAY	SATURDAY	SUNDAY
☐	☐	☐	☐	☐	☐	☐

MONDAY	TUESDAY	WEDNESDAY	THURSDAY	FRIDAY	SATURDAY	SUNDAY
☐	☐	☐	☐	☐	☐	☐

NOTES

MONTHLY GOALS

Month:

10 Goals	The 2 most important. Why?
1.	1º
2.	
3.	
4.	
5.	Deadline:
6.	2º
7.	
8.	
9.	
10.	Deadline:

WEEK: _____	MONDAY	TUESDAY	WEDNESDAY
Goal	Goal	Goal	Goal
SECUNDARY TASKS	Priorities	Priorities	Priorities
	1............................	1............................	1............................
	2............................	2............................	2............................
	3............................	3............................	.
	.		3............................
	6:00........................	6:0	6:00........................
	7:00........................	7:0	7:00........................
	8:00........................	8:0	8:00........................
	9:00........................	9:0	9:00........................
	10:00......................	10:0	10:00......................
ADITIONAL TASKS	11:00......................	11:0	11:00......................
	12:00......................	12:0	12:00......................
	1:00........................	1:00........................	1:00........................
	2:00........................	2:00........................	2:00........................
	3:00........................	3:00........................	3:00........................
	4:00........................	4:00........................	4:00........................
	5:00........................	5:00........................	5:00........................
	6:00........................	6:00........................	6:00........................
	7:00........................	7:00........................	7:00........................
	8:00........................	8:00........................	8:00........................
	9:00........................	9:00........................	9:00........................
	10:00......................	10:00......................	10:00......................
	11:00......................	11:00......................	11:00......................
	12:00......................	12:00......................	12:00......................

HABIT TRACKER			M	T	W	T	F	S	S

THURSDAY	FRIDAY	SATURDAY	SUNDAY
Goal	Goal	Goal	Goal
Priorities	Priorities	Priorities	Priorities
1.........................	1.........................	1.........................	1.........................
2.........................	2.........................	2.........................	2.........................
.	.	.	.
3.........................	3.........................	3.........................	3.........................
6:00....................	6:00....................	6:00....................	6:00....................
7:00....................	7:00....................	7:00....................	7:00....................
8:00....................	8:00....................	8:00....................	8:00....................
9:00....................	9:00....................	9:00....................	9:00....................
10:00..................	10:00..................	10:00..................	10:00..................
11:00..................	11:00..................	11:00..................	11:00..................
12:00..................	12:00..................	12:00..................	12:00..................
1:00....................	1:00....................	1:00....................	1:00....................
2:00....................	2:00....................	2:00....................	2:00....................
3:00....................	3:00....................	3:00....................	3:00....................
4:00....................	4:00....................	4:00....................	4:00....................
5:00....................	5:00....................	5:00....................	5:00....................
6:00....................	6:00....................	6:00....................	6:00....................
7:00....................	7:00....................	7:00....................	7:00....................
8:00....................	8:00....................	8:00....................	8:00....................
9:00....................	9:00....................	9:00....................	9:00....................
10:00..................	10:00..................	10:00..................	10:00..................
11:00..................	11:00..................	11:00..................	11:00..................
12:00	12:00..................	12:00..................	12:00..................

MILESTONES REACHED

REFLECTION ON LAST WEEK

BIGGEST WINS OF LAST WEEK	THINGS TO BE GRATEFUL FOR
IDENTIFY TIME WASTERS	...AND HOW TO REDUCE AND ELIMINATE THEM
SELF-IMPROVEMENT IDEAS	GOALS FOR THE WEEK AHEAD

REWARD FOR HITTING GOALS

What worked?

What didn't work?

What needs improving?

What are my next actions?

WEEK: _____	MONDAY	TUESDAY	WEDNESDAY
Goal	Goal	Goal	Goal
SECUNDARY TASKS	Priorities	Priorities	Priorities

SECUNDARY TASKS	Priorities	Priorities	Priorities
	1.............................	1.............................	1.............................
	2.............................	2.............................	2.............................
	.3............................	3.............................	.
	.		3.............................
	6:00.........................	6:0	6:00.........................
	7:00.........................	7:0	7:00.........................
	8:00.........................	8:0	8:00.........................
	9:00.........................	9:0	9:00.........................
	10:00.......................	10:0	10:00.......................
ADITIONAL TASKS	11:00.......................	11:0	11:00.......................
	12:00.......................	12:0	12:00.......................
	1:00.........................	1:00.........................	1:00.........................
	2:00.........................	2:00.........................	2:00.........................
	.3:00........................	3:00.........................	3:00.........................
	4:00.........................	4:00.........................	4:00.........................
	5:00.........................	5:00.........................	5:00.........................
	6:00.........................	6:00.........................	6:00.........................
	7:00.........................	7:00.........................	7:00.........................
	8:00.........................	8:00.........................	8:00.........................
	9:00.........................	9:00.........................	9:00.........................
	10:00.......................	10:00.......................	10:00.......................
	11:00.......................	11:00.......................	11:00.......................
	12:00.......................	12:00.......................	12:00.......................

HABIT TRACKER	M	T	W	T	F	S	S

THURSDAY	FRIDAY	SATURDAY	SUNDAY
Goal	Goal	Goal	Goal
Priorities	Priorities	Priorities	Priorities
1...	1...	1...	1...
2...	2...	2...	2...
.	.	.	.
3...	3...	3...	3...
6:00.....................................	6:00.....................................	6:00.....................................	6:00.....................................
7:00.....................................	7:00.....................................	7:00.....................................	7:00.....................................
8:00.....................................	8:00.....................................	8:00.....................................	8:00.....................................
9:00.....................................	9:00.....................................	9:00.....................................	9:00.....................................
10:00...................................	10:00...................................	10:00...................................	10:00...................................
11:00...................................	11:00...................................	11:00...................................	11:00...................................
12:00...................................	12:00...................................	12:00...................................	12:00...................................
1:00.....................................	1:00.....................................	1:00.....................................	1:00.....................................
2:00.....................................	2:00.....................................	2:00.....................................	2:00.....................................
3:00.....................................	3:00.....................................	3:00.....................................	3:00.....................................
4:00.....................................	4:00.....................................	4:00.....................................	4:00.....................................
5:00.....................................	5:00.....................................	5:00.....................................	5:00.....................................
6:00.....................................	6:00.....................................	6:00.....................................	6:00.....................................
7:00.....................................	7:00.....................................	7:00.....................................	7:00.....................................
8:00.....................................	8:00.....................................	8:00.....................................	8:00.....................................
9:00.....................................	9:00.....................................	9:00.....................................	9:00.....................................
10:00...................................	10:00...................................	10:00...................................	10:00...................................
11:00...................................	11:00...................................	11:00...................................	11:00...................................
12:00	12:00...................................	12:00...................................	12:00...................................

MILESTONES REACHED

REFLECTION ON LAST WEEK

BIGGEST WINS OF LAST WEEK	THINGS TO BE GRATEFUL FOR
IDENTIFY TIME WASTERS	...AND HOW TO REDUCE AND ELIMINATE THEM
SELF-IMPROVEMENT IDEAS	GOALS FOR THE WEEK AHEAD

REWARD FOR HITTING GOALS

What worked?

What didn't work?

What needs improving?

What are my next actions?

WEEK: _____	MONDAY	TUESDAY	WEDNESDAY
Goal	Goal	Goal	Goal
SECUNDARY TASKS	Priorities	Priorities	Priorities

SECUNDARY TASKS	Priorities	Priorities	Priorities
	1............................	1............................	1............................
	2............................	2............................	2............................
	.3...........................	3............................	.
	.		3............................
	6:00.......................	6:0	6:00.......................
	7:00.......................	7:0	7:00.......................
	8:00.......................	8:0	8:00.......................
	9:00.......................	9:0	9:00.......................
	10:00.....................	10:0	10:00.....................
ADITIONAL TASKS	11:00.....................	11:0	11:00.....................
	12:00.....................	12:0	12:00.....................
	1:00.......................	1:00.......................	1:00.......................
	2:00.......................	2:00.......................	2:00.......................
	.3:00......................	3:00.......................	3:00.......................
	4:00.......................	4:00.......................	4:00.......................
	5:00.......................	5:00.......................	5:00.......................
	6:00.......................	6:00.......................	6:00.......................
	7:00.......................	7:00.......................	7:00.......................
	8:00.......................	8:00.......................	8:00.......................
	9:00.......................	9:00.......................	9:00.......................
	10:00.....................	10:00.....................	10:00.....................
	11:00.....................	11:00.....................	11:00.....................
	12:00.....................	12:00.....................	12:00.....................

HABIT TRACKER		M	T	W	T	F	S	S

THURSDAY	FRIDAY	SATURDAY	SUNDAY
Goal	Goal	Goal	Goal
Priorities	Priorities	Priorities	Priorities
1...............................	1...............................	1...............................	1...............................
2...............................	2...............................	2...............................	2...............................
.	.	.	.
3...............................	3...............................	3...............................	3...............................
6:00............................	6:00............................	6:00............................	6:00............................
7:00............................	7:00............................	7:00............................	7:00............................
8:00............................	8:00............................	8:00............................	8:00............................
9:00............................	9:00............................	9:00............................	9:00............................
10:00..........................	10:00..........................	10:00..........................	10:00..........................
11:00..........................	11:00..........................	11:00..........................	11:00..........................
12:00..........................	12:00..........................	12:00..........................	12:00..........................
1:00............................	1:00............................	1:00............................	1:00............................
2:00............................	2:00............................	2:00............................	2:00............................
3:00............................	3:00............................	3:00............................	3:00............................
4:00............................	4:00............................	4:00............................	4:00............................
5:00............................	5:00............................	5:00............................	5:00............................
6:00............................	6:00............................	6:00............................	6:00............................
7:00............................	7:00............................	7:00............................	7:00............................
8:00............................	8:00............................	8:00............................	8:00............................
9:00............................	9:00............................	9:00............................	9:00............................
10:00..........................	10:00..........................	10:00..........................	10:00..........................
11:00..........................	11:00..........................	11:00..........................	11:00..........................
12:00	12:00..........................	12:00..........................	12:00..........................

MILESTONES REACHED

REFLECTION ON LAST WEEK

BIGGEST WINS OF LAST WEEK	THINGS TO BE GRATEFUL FOR
IDENTIFY TIME WASTERS	...AND HOW TO REDUCE AND ELIMINATE THEM
SELF-IMPROVEMENT IDEAS	GOALS FOR THE WEEK AHEAD

REWARD FOR HITTING GOALS

What worked?

What didn't work?

What needs improving?

What are my next actions?

WEEK: _____	MONDAY	TUESDAY	WEDNESDAY
Goal	Goal	Goal	Goal
SECUNDARY TASKS	Priorities	Priorities	Priorities
	1...............................	1...............................	1...............................
	2...............................	2...............................	2...............................
	3...............................	3...............................	.
	.		3...............................
	6:00...............................	6:0	6:00...............................
	7:00...............................	7:0	7:00...............................
	8:00...............................	8:0	8:00...............................
	9:00...............................	9:0	9:00...............................
	10:00...............................	10:0	10:00...............................
ADITIONAL TASKS	11:00...............................	11:0	11:00...............................
	12:00...............................	12:0	12:00...............................
	1:00...............................	1:00...............................	1:00...............................
	2:00...............................	2:00...............................	2:00...............................
	3:00...............................	3:00...............................	3:00...............................
	4:00...............................	4:00...............................	4:00...............................
	5:00...............................	5:00...............................	5:00...............................
	6:00...............................	6:00...............................	6:00...............................
	7:00...............................	7:00...............................	7:00...............................
	8:00...............................	8:00...............................	8:00...............................
	9:00...............................	9:00...............................	9:00...............................
	10:00...............................	10:00...............................	10:00...............................
	11:00...............................	11:00...............................	11:00...............................
	12:00...............................	12:00...............................	12:00...............................

HABIT TRACKER			M	T	W	T	F	S	S

THURSDAY	FRIDAY	SATURDAY	SUNDAY
Goal	Goal	Goal	Goal
Priorities	Priorities	Priorities	Priorities
1............................	1............................	1............................	1............................
2............................	2............................	2............................	2............................
.	.	.	.
3............................	3............................	3............................	3............................
6:00........................	6:00........................	6:00........................	6:00........................
7:00........................	7:00........................	7:00........................	7:00........................
8:00........................	8:00........................	8:00........................	8:00........................
9:00........................	9:00........................	9:00........................	9:00........................
10:00......................	10:00......................	10:00......................	10:00......................
11:00......................	11:00......................	11:00......................	11:00......................
12:00......................	12:00......................	12:00......................	12:00......................
1:00........................	1:00........................	1:00........................	1:00........................
2:00........................	2:00........................	2:00........................	2:00........................
3:00........................	3:00........................	3:00........................	3:00........................
4:00........................	4:00........................	4:00........................	4:00........................
5:00........................	5:00........................	5:00........................	5:00........................
6:00........................	6:00........................	6:00........................	6:00........................
7:00........................	7:00........................	7:00........................	7:00........................
8:00........................	8:00........................	8:00........................	8:00........................
9:00........................	9:00........................	9:00........................	9:00........................
10:00......................	10:00......................	10:00......................	10:00......................
11:00......................	11:00......................	11:00......................	11:00......................
12:00	12:00......................	12:00......................	12:00......................

MILESTONES REACHED

REFLECTION ON LAST WEEK

BIGGEST WINS OF LAST WEEK	THINGS TO BE GRATEFUL FOR
IDENTIFY TIME WASTERS	...AND HOW TO REDUCE AND ELIMINATE THEM
SELF-IMPROVEMENT IDEAS	GOALS FOR THE WEEK AHEAD

REWARD FOR HITTING GOALS

What worked?

What didn't work?

What needs improving?

What are my next actions?

FEBRUARY

MONTH: _____

MONDAY	TUESDAY	WEDNESDAY	THURSDAY	FRIDAY	SATURDAY	SUNDAY
☐	☐	☐	☐	☐	☐	☐

MONDAY	TUESDAY	WEDNESDAY	THURSDAY	FRIDAY	SATURDAY	SUNDAY
☐	☐	☐	☐	☐	☐	☐

MONDAY	TUESDAY	WEDNESDAY	THURSDAY	FRIDAY	SATURDAY	SUNDAY
☐	☐	☐	☐	☐	☐	☐

MONDAY	TUESDAY	WEDNESDAY	THURSDAY	FRIDAY	SATURDAY	SUNDAY
☐	☐	☐	☐	☐	☐	☐

NOTES

MONTHLY GOALS

Month:

10 Goals	The 2 most important. Why?
1.	**1º**
2.	
3.	
4.	
5.	Deadline:
6.	**2º**
7.	
8.	
9.	
10.	Deadline:

WEEK: _____	MONDAY	TUESDAY	WEDNESDAY
Goal	Goal	Goal	Goal
SECUNDARY TASKS	Priorities	Priorities	Priorities
	1..............................	1..............................	1..............................
	2..............................	2..............................	2..............................
	.3.............................	3..............................	.
	.		3..............................
	6:00..........................	6:0	6:00..........................
	7:00..........................	7:0	7:00..........................
	8:00..........................	8:0	8:00..........................
	9:00..........................	9:0	9:00..........................
	10:00........................	10:0	10:00........................
ADITIONAL TASKS	11:00........................	11:0	11:00........................
	12:00........................	12:0	12:00........................
	1:00..........................	1:00..........................	1:00..........................
	2:00..........................	2:00..........................	2:00..........................
	.3:00.........................	3:00..........................	3:00..........................
	4:00..........................	4:00..........................	4:00..........................
	5:00..........................	5:00..........................	5:00..........................
	6:00..........................	6:00..........................	6:00..........................
	7:00..........................	7:00..........................	7:00..........................
	8:00..........................	8:00..........................	8:00..........................
	9:00..........................	9:00..........................	9:00..........................
	10:00........................	10:00........................	10:00........................
	11:00........................	11:00........................	11:00........................
	12:00........................	12:00........................	12:00........................

HABIT TRACKER	M	T	W	T	F	S	S

THURSDAY	FRIDAY	SATURDAY	SUNDAY
Goal	Goal	Goal	Goal
Priorities	Priorities	Priorities	Priorities
1.........................	1.........................	1.........................	1.........................
2.........................	2.........................	2.........................	2.........................
.	.	.	.
3.........................	3.........................	3.........................	3.........................
6:00....................	6:00....................	6:00....................	6:00....................
7:00....................	7:00....................	7:00....................	7:00....................
8:00....................	8:00....................	8:00....................	8:00....................
9:00....................	9:00....................	9:00....................	9:00....................
10:00..................	10:00..................	10:00..................	10:00..................
11:00..................	11:00..................	11:00..................	11:00..................
12:00..................	12:00..................	12:00..................	12:00..................
1:00....................	1:00....................	1:00....................	1:00....................
2:00....................	2:00....................	2:00....................	2:00....................
3:00....................	3:00....................	3:00....................	3:00....................
4:00....................	4:00....................	4:00....................	4:00....................
5:00....................	5:00....................	5:00....................	5:00....................
6:00....................	6:00....................	6:00....................	6:00....................
7:00....................	7:00....................	7:00....................	7:00....................
8:00....................	8:00....................	8:00....................	8:00....................
9:00....................	9:00....................	9:00....................	9:00....................
10:00..................	10:00..................	10:00..................	10:00..................
11:00..................	11:00..................	11:00..................	11:00..................
12:00	12:00..................	12:00..................	12:00..................

MILESTONES REACHED

REFLECTION ON LAST WEEK

BIGGEST WINS OF LAST WEEK	THINGS TO BE GRATEFUL FOR
IDENTIFY TIME WASTERS	...AND HOW TO REDUCE AND ELIMINATE THEM
SELF-IMPROVEMENT IDEAS	GOALS FOR THE WEEK AHEAD

REWARD FOR HITTING GOALS

What worked?

What didn't work?

What needs improving?

What are my next actions?

WEEK: _____	MONDAY	TUESDAY	WEDNESDAY
Goal	Goal	Goal	Goal
SECUNDARY TASKS	Priorities	Priorities	Priorities
	1..	1..	1..
	2..	2..	2..
	3..	3..	.
	.		3..
	6:00....................................	6:0	6:00....................................
	7:00....................................	7:0	7:00....................................
	8:00....................................	8:0	8:00....................................
	9:00....................................	9:0	9:00....................................
	10:00..................................	10:0	10:00..................................
ADITIONAL TASKS	11:00..................................	11:0	11:00..................................
	12:00..................................	12:0	12:00..................................
	1:00....................................	1:00....................................	1:00....................................
	2:00....................................	2:00....................................	2:00....................................
	3:00....................................	3:00....................................	3:00....................................
	4:00....................................	4:00....................................	4:00....................................
	5:00....................................	5:00....................................	5:00....................................
	6:00....................................	6:00....................................	6:00....................................
	7:00....................................	7:00....................................	7:00....................................
	8:00....................................	8:00....................................	8:00....................................
	9:00....................................	9:00....................................	9:00....................................
	10:00..................................	10:00..................................	10:00..................................
	11:00..................................	11:00..................................	11:00..................................
	12:00..................................	12:00..................................	12:00..................................

HABIT TRACKER		M	T	W	T	F	S	S

THURSDAY	FRIDAY	SATURDAY	SUNDAY
Goal	Goal	Goal	Goal
Priorities	Priorities	Priorities	Priorities
1...	1...	1...	1...
2...	2...	2...	2...
.	.	.	.
3...	3...	3...	3...
6:00..	6:00..	6:00..	6:00..
7:00..	7:00..	7:00..	7:00..
8:00..	8:00..	8:00..	8:00..
9:00..	9:00..	9:00..	9:00..
10:00..	10:00..	10:00..	10:00..
11:00..	11:00..	11:00..	11:00..
12:00..	12:00..	12:00..	12:00..
1:00..	1:00..	1:00..	1:00..
2:00..	2:00..	2:00..	2:00..
3:00..	3:00..	3:00..	3:00..
4:00..	4:00..	4:00..	4:00..
5:00..	5:00..	5:00..	5:00..
6:00..	6:00..	6:00..	6:00..
7:00..	7:00..	7:00..	7:00..
8:00..	8:00..	8:00..	8:00..
9:00..	9:00..	9:00..	9:00..
10:00..	10:00..	10:00..	10:00..
11:00..	11:00..	11:00..	11:00..
12:00	12:00	12:00	12:00 ....

MILESTONES REACHED

REFLECTION ON LAST WEEK

BIGGEST WINS OF LAST WEEK	THINGS TO BE GRATEFUL FOR
IDENTIFY TIME WASTERS	...AND HOW TO REDUCE AND ELIMINATE THEM
SELF-IMPROVEMENT IDEAS	GOALS FOR THE WEEK AHEAD

REWARD FOR HITTING GOALS

What worked?

What didn't work?

What needs improving?

What are my next actions?

WEEK: _____	MONDAY	TUESDAY	WEDNESDAY
Goal	Goal	Goal	Goal
SECUNDARY TASKS	Priorities	Priorities	Priorities
	1............................	1............................	1............................
	2............................	2............................	2............................
	.3............................	3............................	.
	.		3............................
	6:00............................	6:0	6:00............................
	7:00............................	7:0	7:00............................
	8:00............................	8:0	8:00............................
	9:00............................	9:0	9:00............................
	10:00............................	10:0	10:00............................
ADITIONAL TASKS	11:00............................	11:0	11:00............................
	12:00............................	12:0	12:00............................
	1:00............................	1:00............................	1:00............................
	2:00............................	2:00............................	2:00............................
	.3:00............................	3:00............................	3:00............................
	4:00............................	4:00............................	4:00............................
	5:00............................	5:00............................	5:00............................
	6:00............................	6:00............................	6:00............................
	7:00............................	7:00............................	7:00............................
	8:00............................	8:00............................	8:00............................
	9:00............................	9:00............................	9:00............................
	10:00............................	10:00............................	10:00............................
	11:00............................	11:00............................	11:00............................
	12:00............................	12:00............................	12:00............................

HABIT TRACKER	M	T	W	T	F	S	S

THURSDAY	FRIDAY	SATURDAY	SUNDAY
Goal	Goal	Goal	Goal
Priorities	Priorities	Priorities	Priorities
1..........................	1..........................	1..........................	1..........................
2..........................	2..........................	2..........................	2..........................
.	.	.	.
3..........................	3..........................	3..........................	3..........................
6:00..........................	6:00..........................	6:00..........................	6:00..........................
7:00..........................	7:00..........................	7:00..........................	7:00..........................
8:00..........................	8:00..........................	8:00..........................	8:00..........................
9:00..........................	9:00..........................	9:00..........................	9:00..........................
10:00..........................	10:00..........................	10:00..........................	10:00..........................
11:00..........................	11:00..........................	11:00..........................	11:00..........................
12:00..........................	12:00..........................	12:00..........................	12:00..........................
1:00..........................	1:00..........................	1:00..........................	1:00..........................
2:00..........................	2:00..........................	2:00..........................	2:00..........................
3:00..........................	3:00..........................	3:00..........................	3:00..........................
4:00..........................	4:00..........................	4:00..........................	4:00..........................
5:00..........................	5:00..........................	5:00..........................	5:00..........................
6:00..........................	6:00..........................	6:00..........................	6:00..........................
7:00..........................	7:00..........................	7:00..........................	7:00..........................
8:00..........................	8:00..........................	8:00..........................	8:00..........................
9:00..........................	9:00..........................	9:00..........................	9:00..........................
10:00..........................	10:00..........................	10:00..........................	10:00..........................
11:00..........................	11:00..........................	11:00..........................	11:00..........................
12:00	12:00..........................	12:00..........................	12:00..........................

MILESTONES REACHED

REFLECTION ON LAST WEEK

BIGGEST WINS OF LAST WEEK	THINGS TO BE GRATEFUL FOR
IDENTIFY TIME WASTERS	...AND HOW TO REDUCE AND ELIMINATE THEM
SELF-IMPROVEMENT IDEAS	GOALS FOR THE WEEK AHEAD

REWARD FOR HITTING GOALS

What worked?

What didn't work?

What needs improving?

What are my next actions?

WEEK: _____	MONDAY	TUESDAY	WEDNESDAY
Goal	Goal	Goal	Goal
SECUNDARY TASKS	Priorities	Priorities	Priorities
	1..............................	1..............................	1..............................
	2..............................	2..............................	2..............................
	3..............................	3..............................	.
	.		3..............................
	6:00..........................	6:0	6:00..........................
	7:00..........................	7:0	7:00..........................
	8:00..........................	8:0	8:00..........................
	9:00..........................	9:0	9:00..........................
	10:00........................	10:0	10:00........................
ADITIONAL TASKS	11:00........................	11:0	11:00........................
	12:00........................	12:0	12:00........................
	1:00..........................	1:00..........................	1:00..........................
	2:00..........................	2:00..........................	2:00..........................
	.3:00.........................	3:00..........................	3:00..........................
	4:00..........................	4:00..........................	4:00..........................
	5:00..........................	5:00..........................	5:00..........................
	6:00..........................	6:00..........................	6:00..........................
	7:00..........................	7:00..........................	7:00..........................
	8:00..........................	8:00..........................	8:00..........................
	9:00..........................	9:00..........................	9:00..........................
	10:00........................	10:00........................	10:00........................
	11:00........................	11:00........................	11:00........................
	12:00........................	12:00........................	12:00........................

HABIT TRACKER			M	T	W	T	F	S	S

THURSDAY	FRIDAY	SATURDAY	SUNDAY
Goal	Goal	Goal	Goal
Priorities	Priorities	Priorities	Priorities
1..........................	1..........................	1..........................	1..........................
2..........................	2..........................	2..........................	2..........................
.	.	.	.
3..........................	3..........................	3..........................	3..........................
6:00..........................	6:00..........................	6:00..........................	6:00..........................
7:00..........................	7:00..........................	7:00..........................	7:00..........................
8:00..........................	8:00..........................	8:00..........................	8:00..........................
9:00..........................	9:00..........................	9:00..........................	9:00..........................
10:00..........................	10:00..........................	10:00..........................	10:00..........................
11:00..........................	11:00..........................	11:00..........................	11:00..........................
12:00..........................	12:00..........................	12:00..........................	12:00..........................
1:00..........................	1:00..........................	1:00..........................	1:00..........................
2:00..........................	2:00..........................	2:00..........................	2:00..........................
3:00..........................	3:00..........................	3:00..........................	3:00..........................
4:00..........................	4:00..........................	4:00..........................	4:00..........................
5:00..........................	5:00..........................	5:00..........................	5:00..........................
6:00..........................	6:00..........................	6:00..........................	6:00..........................
7:00..........................	7:00..........................	7:00..........................	7:00..........................
8:00..........................	8:00..........................	8:00..........................	8:00..........................
9:00..........................	9:00..........................	9:00..........................	9:00..........................
10:00..........................	10:00..........................	10:00..........................	10:00..........................
11:00..........................	11:00..........................	11:00..........................	11:00..........................
12:00	12:00..........................	12:00..........................	12:00..........................

MILESTONES REACHED

REFLECTION ON LAST WEEK

BIGGEST WINS OF LAST WEEK	THINGS TO BE GRATEFUL FOR
IDENTIFY TIME WASTERS	...AND HOW TO REDUCE AND ELIMINATE THEM
SELF-IMPROVEMENT IDEAS	GOALS FOR THE WEEK AHEAD

REWARD FOR HITTING GOALS

What worked?

What didn't work?

What needs improving?

What are my next actions?

"Productivity is never an accident. It is always the result of a commitment to excellence, intelligent planning, and focused effort."

Paul J. Meyer

MARCH

MONDAY	TUESDAY	WEDNESDAY	THURSDAY	FRIDAY	SATURDAY	SUNDAY
☐	☐	☐	☐	☐	☐	☐

MONDAY	TUESDAY	WEDNESDAY	THURSDAY	FRIDAY	SATURDAY	SUNDAY
☐	☐	☐	☐	☐	☐	☐

MONDAY	TUESDAY	WEDNESDAY	THURSDAY	FRIDAY	SATURDAY	SUNDAY
☐	☐	☐	☐	☐	☐	☐

MONDAY	TUESDAY	WEDNESDAY	THURSDAY	FRIDAY	SATURDAY	SUNDAY
☐	☐	☐	☐	☐	☐	☐

NOTES

MONTHLY GOALS

Month:

10 Goals	The 2 most important. Why?
1.	**1º**
2.	
3.	
4.	
5.	Deadline:
6.	**2º**
7.	
8.	
9.	
10.	Deadline:

WEEK: _____	MONDAY	TUESDAY	WEDNESDAY
Goal	Goal	Goal	Goal
SECUNDARY TASKS	Priorities	Priorities	Priorities
	1.............................	1.............................	1.............................
	2.............................	2.............................	2.............................
	.3............................	3.............................	.
	.		3.............................
	6:00..........................	6:0	6:00..........................
	7:00..........................	7:0	7:00..........................
	8:00..........................	8:0	8:00..........................
	9:00..........................	9:0	9:00..........................
	10:00........................	10:0	10:00........................
ADITIONAL TASKS	11:00........................	11:0	11:00........................
	12:00........................	12:0	12:00........................
	1:00..........................	1:00..........................	1:00..........................
	2:00..........................	2:00..........................	2:00..........................
	.3:00.........................	3:00..........................	3:00..........................
	4:00..........................	4:00..........................	4:00..........................
	5:00..........................	5:00..........................	5:00..........................
	6:00..........................	6:00..........................	6:00..........................
	7:00..........................	7:00..........................	7:00..........................
	8:00..........................	8:00..........................	8:00..........................
	9:00..........................	9:00..........................	9:00..........................
	10:00........................	10:00........................	10:00........................
	11:00........................	11:00........................	11:00........................
	12:00........................	12:00........................	12:00........................

HABIT TRACKER	M	T	W	T	F	S	S

THURSDAY	FRIDAY	SATURDAY	SUNDAY
Goal	Goal	Goal	Goal
Priorities	Priorities	Priorities	Priorities
1.......................	1.......................	1.......................	1.......................
2.......................	2.......................	2.......................	2.......................
.	.	.	.
3.......................	3.......................	3.......................	3.......................
6:00.......................	6:00.......................	6:00.......................	6:00.......................
7:00.......................	7:00.......................	7:00.......................	7:00.......................
8:00.......................	8:00.......................	8:00.......................	8:00.......................
9:00.......................	9:00.......................	9:00.......................	9:00.......................
10:00.......................	10:00.......................	10:00.......................	10:00.......................
11:00.......................	11:00.......................	11:00.......................	11:00.......................
12:00.......................	12:00.......................	12:00.......................	12:00.......................
1:00.......................	1:00.......................	1:00.......................	1:00.......................
2:00.......................	2:00.......................	2:00.......................	2:00.......................
3:00.......................	3:00.......................	3:00.......................	3:00.......................
4:00.......................	4:00.......................	4:00.......................	4:00.......................
5:00.......................	5:00.......................	5:00.......................	5:00.......................
6:00.......................	6:00.......................	6:00.......................	6:00.......................
7:00.......................	7:00.......................	7:00.......................	7:00.......................
8:00.......................	8:00.......................	8:00.......................	8:00.......................
9:00.......................	9:00.......................	9:00.......................	9:00.......................
10:00.......................	10:00.......................	10:00.......................	10:00.......................
11:00.......................	11:00.......................	11:00.......................	11:00.......................
12:00	12:00.......................	12:00.......................	12:00.......................

MILESTONES REACHED

REFLECTION ON LAST WEEK

BIGGEST WINS OF LAST WEEK	THINGS TO BE GRATEFUL FOR
IDENTIFY TIME WASTERS	...AND HOW TO REDUCE AND ELIMINATE THEM
SELF-IMPROVEMENT IDEAS	GOALS FOR THE WEEK AHEAD

REWARD FOR HITTING GOALS

What worked?

What didn't work?

What needs improving?

What are my next actions?

WEEK: _____	MONDAY	TUESDAY	WEDNESDAY
Goal	**Goal**	**Goal**	**Goal**
SECUNDARY TASKS	**Priorities**	**Priorities**	**Priorities**
	1.............................	1.............................	1.............................
	2.............................	2.............................	2.............................
	3.............................	3.............................	.
	.		3.............................
	6:00........................	6:0	6:00........................
	7:00........................	7:0	7:00........................
	8:00........................	8:0	8:00........................
	9:00........................	9:0	9:00........................
	10:00......................	10:0	10:00......................
ADITIONAL TASKS	11:00......................	11:0	11:00......................
	12:00......................	12:0	12:00......................
	1:00........................	1:00........................	1:00........................
	2:00........................	2:00........................	2:00........................
	.3:00.......................	3:00........................	3:00........................
	4:00........................	4:00........................	4:00........................
	5:00........................	5:00........................	5:00........................
	6:00........................	6:00........................	6:00........................
	7:00........................	7:00........................	7:00........................
	8:00........................	8:00........................	8:00........................
	9:00........................	9:00........................	9:00........................
	10:00......................	10:00......................	10:00......................
	11:00......................	11:00......................	11:00......................
	12:00......................	12:00......................	12:00......................

HABIT TRACKER	M	T	W	T	F	S	S

THURSDAY	FRIDAY	SATURDAY	SUNDAY
Goal	Goal	Goal	Goal
Priorities	Priorities	Priorities	Priorities
1...	1...	1...	1...
2...	2...	2...	2...
.	.	.	.
3...	3...	3...	3...
6:00...	6:00...	6:00...	6:00...
7:00...	7:00...	7:00...	7:00...
8:00...	8:00...	8:00...	8:00...
9:00...	9:00...	9:00...	9:00...
10:00...	10:00...	10:00...	10:00...
11:00...	11:00...	11:00...	11:00...
12:00...	12:00...	12:00...	12:00...
1:00...	1:00...	1:00...	1:00...
2:00...	2:00...	2:00...	2:00...
3:00...	3:00...	3:00...	3:00...
4:00...	4:00...	4:00...	4:00...
5:00...	5:00...	5:00...	5:00...
6:00...	6:00...	6:00...	6:00...
7:00...	7:00...	7:00...	7:00...
8:00...	8:00...	8:00...	8:00...
9:00...	9:00...	9:00...	9:00...
10:00...	10:00...	10:00...	10:00...
11:00...	11:00...	11:00...	11:00...
12:00	12:00...	12:00...	12:00...

MILESTONES REACHED

REFLECTION ON LAST WEEK

BIGGEST WINS OF LAST WEEK	THINGS TO BE GRATEFUL FOR
IDENTIFY TIME WASTERS	...AND HOW TO REDUCE AND ELIMINATE THEM
SELF-IMPROVEMENT IDEAS	GOALS FOR THE WEEK AHEAD

REWARD FOR HITTING GOALS

What worked?

What didn't work?

What needs improving?

What are my next actions?

WEEK: _____	MONDAY	TUESDAY	WEDNESDAY
Goal	Goal	Goal	Goal
SECUNDARY TASKS	Priorities	Priorities	Priorities

SECUNDARY TASKS	Priorities	Priorities	Priorities
	1..	1..	1..
	2..	2..	2..
	3..	3..	.
	.		3..
	6:00....................................	6:0	6:00....................................
	7:00....................................	7:0	7:00....................................
	8:00....................................	8:0	8:00....................................
	9:00....................................	9:0	9:00....................................
	10:00..................................	10:0	10:00..................................
ADITIONAL TASKS	11:00..................................	11:0	11:00..................................
	12:00..................................	12:0	12:00..................................
	1:00....................................	1:00....................................	1:00....................................
	2:00....................................	2:00....................................	2:00....................................
	.3:00....................................	3:00....................................	3:00....................................
	4:00....................................	4:00....................................	4:00....................................
	5:00....................................	5:00....................................	5:00....................................
	6:00....................................	6:00....................................	6:00....................................
	7:00....................................	7:00....................................	7:00....................................
	8:00....................................	8:00....................................	8:00....................................
	9:00....................................	9:00....................................	9:00....................................
	10:00..................................	10:00..................................	10:00..................................
	11:00..................................	11:00..................................	11:00..................................
	12:00..................................	12:00..................................	12:00..................................

HABIT TRACKER		M	T	W	T	F	S	S

THURSDAY	FRIDAY	SATURDAY	SUNDAY
Goal	Goal	Goal	Goal
Priorities	Priorities	Priorities	Priorities
1...	1...	1...	1...
2...	2...	2...	2...
.	.	.	.
3...	3...	3...	3...
6:00...	6:00...	6:00...	6:00...
7:00...	7:00...	7:00...	7:00...
8:00...	8:00...	8:00...	8:00...
9:00...	9:00...	9:00...	9:00...
10:00...	10:00...	10:00...	10:00...
11:00...	11:00...	11:00...	11:00...
12:00...	12:00...	12:00...	12:00...
1:00...	1:00...	1:00...	1:00...
2:00...	2:00...	2:00...	2:00...
3:00...	3:00...	3:00...	3:00...
4:00...	4:00...	4:00...	4:00...
5:00...	5:00...	5:00...	5:00...
6:00...	6:00...	6:00...	6:00...
7:00...	7:00...	7:00...	7:00...
8:00...	8:00...	8:00...	8:00...
9:00...	9:00...	9:00...	9:00...
10:00...	10:00...	10:00...	10:00...
11:00...	11:00...	11:00...	11:00...
12:00	12:00...	12:00...	12:00...

MILESTONES REACHED

REFLECTION ON LAST WEEK

BIGGEST WINS OF LAST WEEK	THINGS TO BE GRATEFUL FOR
IDENTIFY TIME WASTERS	...AND HOW TO REDUCE AND ELIMINATE THEM
SELF-IMPROVEMENT IDEAS	GOALS FOR THE WEEK AHEAD

REWARD FOR HITTING GOALS

What worked?

What didn't work?

What needs improving?

What are my next actions?

WEEK: _____	MONDAY	TUESDAY	WEDNESDAY
Goal	Goal	Goal	Goal
SECUNDARY TASKS	Priorities	Priorities	Priorities
	1...............................	1...............................	1...............................
	2...............................	2...............................	2...............................
	.3............................	3...............................	.
	.		3...............................
	6:00...........................	6:0	6:00...........................
	7:00...........................	7:0	7:00...........................
	8:00...........................	8:0	8:00...........................
	9:00...........................	9:0	9:00...........................
	10:00.........................	10:0	10:00.........................
ADITIONAL TASKS	11:00.........................	11:0	11:00.........................
	12:00.........................	12:0	12:00.........................
	1:00...........................	1:00...........................	1:00...........................
	2:00...........................	2:00...........................	2:00...........................
	.3:00..........................	3:00...........................	3:00...........................
	4:00...........................	4:00...........................	4:00...........................
	5:00...........................	5:00...........................	5:00...........................
	6:00...........................	6:00...........................	6:00...........................
	7:00...........................	7:00...........................	7:00...........................
	8:00...........................	8:00...........................	8:00...........................
	9:00...........................	9:00...........................	9:00...........................
	10:00.........................	10:00.........................	10:00.........................
	11:00.........................	11:00.........................	11:00.........................
	12:00.........................	12:00.........................	12:00.........................

HABIT TRACKER		M	T	W	T	F	S	S

THURSDAY	FRIDAY	SATURDAY	SUNDAY
Goal	Goal	Goal	Goal
Priorities	Priorities	Priorities	Priorities
1.........................	1.........................	1.........................	1.........................
2.........................	2.........................	2.........................	2.........................
.	.	.	.
3.........................	3.........................	3.........................	3.........................
6:00.........................	6:00.........................	6:00.........................	6:00.........................
7:00.........................	7:00.........................	7:00.........................	7:00.........................
8:00.........................	8:00.........................	8:00.........................	8:00.........................
9:00.........................	9:00.........................	9:00.........................	9:00.........................
10:00.........................	10:00.........................	10:00.........................	10:00.........................
11:00.........................	11:00.........................	11:00.........................	11:00.........................
12:00.........................	12:00.........................	12:00.........................	12:00.........................
1:00.........................	1:00.........................	1:00.........................	1:00.........................
2:00.........................	2:00.........................	2:00.........................	2:00.........................
3:00.........................	3:00.........................	3:00.........................	3:00.........................
4:00.........................	4:00.........................	4:00.........................	4:00.........................
5:00.........................	5:00.........................	5:00.........................	5:00.........................
6:00.........................	6:00.........................	6:00.........................	6:00.........................
7:00.........................	7:00.........................	7:00.........................	7:00.........................
8:00.........................	8:00.........................	8:00.........................	8:00.........................
9:00.........................	9:00.........................	9:00.........................	9:00.........................
10:00.........................	10:00.........................	10:00.........................	10:00.........................
11:00.........................	11:00.........................	11:00.........................	11:00.........................
12:00	12:00.........................	12:00.........................	12:00.........................

MILESTONES REACHED

REFLECTION ON LAST WEEK

BIGGEST WINS OF LAST WEEK	THINGS TO BE GRATEFUL FOR
IDENTIFY TIME WASTERS	...AND HOW TO REDUCE AND ELIMINATE THEM
SELF-IMPROVEMENT IDEAS	GOALS FOR THE WEEK AHEAD

REWARD FOR HITTING GOALS

What worked?

What didn't work?

What needs improving?

What are my next actions?

"The way to get started is to quit talking and begin doing."

Walt Disney

APRIL

MONDAY	TUESDAY	WEDNESDAY	THURSDAY	FRIDAY	SATURDAY	SUNDAY
☐	☐	☐	☐	☐	☐	☐
MONDAY	TUESDAY	WEDNESDAY	THURSDAY	FRIDAY	SATURDAY	SUNDAY
☐	☐	☐	☐	☐	☐	☐
MONDAY	TUESDAY	WEDNESDAY	THURSDAY	FRIDAY	SATURDAY	SUNDAY
☐	☐	☐	☐	☐	☐	☐
MONDAY	TUESDAY	WEDNESDAY	THURSDAY	FRIDAY	SATURDAY	SUNDAY
☐	☐	☐	☐	☐	☐	☐

NOTES

MONTHLY GOALS

Month:

10 Goals	The 2 most important. Why?
1.	**1º**
2.	
3.	
4.	
5.	Deadline:
6.	**2º**
7.	
8.	
9.	
10.	Deadline:

WEEK: _____	MONDAY	TUESDAY	WEDNESDAY
Goal	Goal	Goal	Goal
		.	
SECUNDARY TASKS	Priorities	Priorities	Priorities
	1....................................	1....................................	1....................................
	2....................................	2....................................	2....................................
	.3....................................	3....................................	.
	.		3....................................
	6:00....................................	6:0	6:00....................................
	7:00....................................	7:0	7:00....................................
	8:00....................................	8:0	8:00....................................
	9:00....................................	9:0	9:00....................................
	10:00....................................	10:0	10:00....................................
ADITIONAL TASKS	11:00....................................	11:0	11:00....................................
	12:00....................................	12:0	12:00....................................
	1:00....................................	1:00....................................	1:00....................................
	2:00....................................	2:00....................................	2:00....................................
	.3:00....................................	3:00....................................	3:00....................................
	4:00....................................	4:00....................................	4:00....................................
	5:00....................................	5:00....................................	5:00....................................
	6:00....................................	6:00....................................	6:00....................................
	7:00....................................	7:00....................................	7:00....................................
	8:00....................................	8:00....................................	8:00....................................
	9:00....................................	9:00....................................	9:00....................................
	10:00....................................	10:00....................................	10:00....................................
	11:00....................................	11:00....................................	11:00....................................
	12:00....................................	12:00....................................	12:00....................................

HABIT TRACKER	M	T	W	T	F	S	S

THURSDAY	FRIDAY	SATURDAY	SUNDAY
Goal	Goal	Goal	Goal
Priorities	Priorities	Priorities	Priorities
1..	1..	1..	1..
2..	2..	2..	2..
.	.	.	.
3..	3..	3..	3..
6:00......................................	6:00......................................	6:00......................................	6:00......................................
7:00......................................	7:00......................................	7:00......................................	7:00......................................
8:00......................................	8:00......................................	8:00......................................	8:00......................................
9:00......................................	9:00......................................	9:00......................................	9:00......................................
10:00....................................	10:00....................................	10:00....................................	10:00....................................
11:00....................................	11:00....................................	11:00....................................	11:00....................................
12:00....................................	12:00....................................	12:00....................................	12:00....................................
1:00......................................	1:00......................................	1:00......................................	1:00......................................
2:00......................................	2:00......................................	2:00......................................	2:00......................................
3:00......................................	3:00......................................	3:00......................................	3:00......................................
4:00......................................	4:00......................................	4:00......................................	4:00......................................
5:00......................................	5:00......................................	5:00......................................	5:00......................................
6:00......................................	6:00......................................	6:00......................................	6:00......................................
7:00......................................	7:00......................................	7:00......................................	7:00......................................
8:00......................................	8:00......................................	8:00......................................	8:00......................................
9:00......................................	9:00......................................	9:00......................................	9:00......................................
10:00....................................	10:00....................................	10:00....................................	10:00....................................
11:00....................................	11:00....................................	11:00....................................	11:00....................................
12:00	12:00....................................	12:00....................................	12:00....................................

MILESTONES REACHED

REFLECTION ON LAST WEEK

BIGGEST WINS OF LAST WEEK	THINGS TO BE GRATEFUL FOR
IDENTIFY TIME WASTERS	...AND HOW TO REDUCE AND ELIMINATE THEM
SELF-IMPROVEMENT IDEAS	GOALS FOR THE WEEK AHEAD

REWARD FOR HITTING GOALS

What worked?

What didn't work?

What needs improving?

What are my next actions?

WEEK: _____	MONDAY	TUESDAY	WEDNESDAY
Goal	Goal	Goal	Goal
SECUNDARY TASKS	Priorities	Priorities	Priorities
	1..	1..	1..
	2..	2..	2..
	.3..	3..	.
	.		3..
	6:00..	6:0	6:00..
	7:00..	7:0	7:00..
	8:00..	8:0	8:00..
	9:00..	9:0	9:00..
	10:00..	10:0	10:00..
ADITIONAL TASKS	11:00..	11:0	11:00..
	12:00..	12:0	12:00..
	1:00..	1:00..	1:00..
	2:00..	2:00..	2:00..
	.3:00..	3:00..	3:00..
	4:00..	4:00..	4:00..
	5:00..	5:00..	5:00..
	6:00..	6:00..	6:00..
	7:00..	7:00..	7:00..
	8:00..	8:00..	8:00..
	9:00..	9:00..	9:00..
	10:00..	10:00..	10:00..
	11:00..	11:00..	11:00..
	12:00..	12:00..	12:00..

HABIT TRACKER			M	T	W	T	F	S	S

THURSDAY	FRIDAY	SATURDAY	SUNDAY
Goal	Goal	Goal	Goal
Priorities	Priorities	Priorities	Priorities
1...................................	1...................................	1...................................	1...................................
2...................................	2...................................	2...................................	2...................................
.	.	.	.
3...................................	3...................................	3...................................	3...................................
6:00................................	6:00................................	6:00................................	6:00................................
7:00................................	7:00................................	7:00................................	7:00................................
8:00................................	8:00................................	8:00................................	8:00................................
9:00................................	9:00................................	9:00................................	9:00................................
10:00..............................	10:00..............................	10:00..............................	10:00..............................
11:00..............................	11:00..............................	11:00..............................	11:00..............................
12:00..............................	12:00..............................	12:00..............................	12:00..............................
1:00................................	1:00................................	1:00................................	1:00................................
2:00................................	2:00................................	2:00................................	2:00................................
3:00................................	3:00................................	3:00................................	3:00................................
4:00................................	4:00................................	4:00................................	4:00................................
5:00................................	5:00................................	5:00................................	5:00................................
6:00................................	6:00................................	6:00................................	6:00................................
7:00................................	7:00................................	7:00................................	7:00................................
8:00................................	8:00................................	8:00................................	8:00................................
9:00................................	9:00................................	9:00................................	9:00................................
10:00..............................	10:00..............................	10:00..............................	10:00..............................
11:00..............................	11:00..............................	11:00..............................	11:00..............................
12:00..............................	12:00..............................	12:00..............................	12:00..............................

MILESTONES REACHED

REFLECTION ON LAST WEEK

BIGGEST WINS OF LAST WEEK	THINGS TO BE GRATEFUL FOR
IDENTIFY TIME WASTERS	...AND HOW TO REDUCE AND ELIMINATE THEM
SELF-IMPROVEMENT IDEAS	GOALS FOR THE WEEK AHEAD

REWARD FOR HITTING GOALS

What worked?

What didn't work?

What needs improving?

What are my next actions?

WEEK: _____	MONDAY	TUESDAY	WEDNESDAY
Goal	Goal	Goal	Goal
SECUNDARY TASKS	Priorities	Priorities	Priorities
	1.............................	1.............................	1.............................
	2.............................	2.............................	2.............................
	.3............................	3.............................	.
	.		3.............................
	6:00.........................	6:0	6:00.........................
	7:00.........................	7:0	7:00.........................
	8:00.........................	8:0	8:00.........................
	9:00.........................	9:0	9:00.........................
	10:00.......................	10:0	10:00.......................
ADITIONAL TASKS	11:00.......................	11:0	11:00.......................
	12:00.......................	12:0	12:00.......................
	1:00.........................	1:00.........................	1:00.........................
	2:00.........................	2:00.........................	2:00.........................
	.3:00........................	3:00.........................	3:00.........................
	4:00.........................	4:00.........................	4:00.........................
	5:00.........................	5:00.........................	5:00.........................
	6:00.........................	6:00.........................	6:00.........................
	7:00.........................	7:00.........................	7:00.........................
	8:00.........................	8:00.........................	8:00.........................
	9:00.........................	9:00.........................	9:00.........................
	10:00.......................	10:00.......................	10:00.......................
	11:00.......................	11:00.......................	11:00.......................
	12:00.......................	12:00.......................	12:00.......................

HABIT TRACKER		M	T	W	T	F	S	S

THURSDAY	FRIDAY	SATURDAY	SUNDAY
Goal	Goal	Goal	Goal
Priorities	Priorities	Priorities	Priorities
1.............................	1.............................	1.............................	1.............................
2.............................	2.............................	2.............................	2.............................
.	.	.	.
3.............................	3.............................	3.............................	3.............................
6:00.........................	6:00.........................	6:00.........................	6:00.........................
7:00.........................	7:00.........................	7:00.........................	7:00.........................
8:00.........................	8:00.........................	8:00.........................	8:00.........................
9:00.........................	9:00.........................	9:00.........................	9:00.........................
10:00.......................	10:00.......................	10:00.......................	10:00.......................
11:00.......................	11:00.......................	11:00.......................	11:00.......................
12:00.......................	12:00.......................	12:00.......................	12:00.......................
1:00.........................	1:00.........................	1:00.........................	1:00.........................
2:00.........................	2:00.........................	2:00.........................	2:00.........................
3:00.........................	3:00.........................	3:00.........................	3:00.........................
4:00.........................	4:00.........................	4:00.........................	4:00.........................
5:00.........................	5:00.........................	5:00.........................	5:00.........................
6:00.........................	6:00.........................	6:00.........................	6:00.........................
7:00.........................	7:00.........................	7:00.........................	7:00.........................
8:00.........................	8:00.........................	8:00.........................	8:00.........................
9:00.........................	9:00.........................	9:00.........................	9:00.........................
10:00.......................	10:00.......................	10:00.......................	10:00.......................
11:00.......................	11:00.......................	11:00.......................	11:00.......................
12:00	12:00.......................	12:00.......................	12:00.......................

MILESTONES REACHED

REFLECTION ON LAST WEEK

BIGGEST WINS OF LAST WEEK	THINGS TO BE GRATEFUL FOR
IDENTIFY TIME WASTERS	...AND HOW TO REDUCE AND ELIMINATE THEM
SELF-IMPROVEMENT IDEAS	GOALS FOR THE WEEK AHEAD

REWARD FOR HITTING GOALS

What worked?

What didn't work?

What needs improving?

What are my next actions?

WEEK: _____	MONDAY	TUESDAY	WEDNESDAY
Goal	Goal	Goal	Goal
SECUNDARY TASKS	Priorities	Priorities	Priorities

	MONDAY	TUESDAY	WEDNESDAY
	1..	1..	1..
	2..	2..	2..
	.3.......................................	3..	.
	.		3..
	6:00....................................	6:0	6:00....................................
	7:00....................................	7:0	7:00....................................
	8:00....................................	8:0	8:00....................................
	9:00....................................	9:0	9:00....................................
	10:00...................................	10:0	10:00...................................
ADITIONAL TASKS	11:00...................................	11:0	11:00...................................
	12:00...................................	12:0	12:00...................................
	1:00....................................	1:00....................................	1:00....................................
	2:00....................................	2:00....................................	2:00....................................
	.3:00....................................	3:00....................................	3:00....................................
	4:00....................................	4:00....................................	4:00....................................
	5:00....................................	5:00....................................	5:00....................................
	6:00....................................	6:00....................................	6:00....................................
	7:00....................................	7:00....................................	7:00....................................
	8:00....................................	8:00....................................	8:00....................................
	9:00....................................	9:00....................................	9:00....................................
	10:00...................................	10:00...................................	10:00...................................
	11:00...................................	11:00...................................	11:00...................................
	12:00...................................	12:00...................................	12:00...................................

HABIT TRACKER			M	T	W	T	F	S	S

THURSDAY	FRIDAY	SATURDAY	SUNDAY
Goal	Goal	Goal	Goal
Priorities	Priorities	Priorities	Priorities
1............................	1............................	1............................	1............................
2............................	2............................	2............................	2............................
.	.	.	.
3............................	3............................	3............................	3............................
6:00.........................	6:00.........................	6:00.........................	6:00.........................
7:00.........................	7:00.........................	7:00.........................	7:00.........................
8:00.........................	8:00.........................	8:00.........................	8:00.........................
9:00.........................	9:00.........................	9:00.........................	9:00.........................
10:00.......................	10:00.......................	10:00.......................	10:00.......................
11:00.......................	11:00.......................	11:00.......................	11:00.......................
12:00.......................	12:00.......................	12:00.......................	12:00.......................
1:00.........................	1:00.........................	1:00.........................	1:00.........................
2:00.........................	2:00.........................	2:00.........................	2:00.........................
3:00.........................	3:00.........................	3:00.........................	3:00.........................
4:00.........................	4:00.........................	4:00.........................	4:00.........................
5:00.........................	5:00.........................	5:00.........................	5:00.........................
6:00.........................	6:00.........................	6:00.........................	6:00.........................
7:00.........................	7:00.........................	7:00.........................	7:00.........................
8:00.........................	8:00.........................	8:00.........................	8:00.........................
9:00.........................	9:00.........................	9:00.........................	9:00.........................
10:00.......................	10:00.......................	10:00.......................	10:00.......................
11:00.......................	11:00.......................	11:00.......................	11:00.......................
12:00	12:00.......................	12:00.......................	12:00.......................

MILESTONES REACHED

REFLECTION ON LAST WEEK

BIGGEST WINS OF LAST WEEK	THINGS TO BE GRATEFUL FOR
IDENTIFY TIME WASTERS	...AND HOW TO REDUCE AND ELIMINATE THEM
SELF-IMPROVEMENT IDEAS	GOALS FOR THE WEEK AHEAD

REWARD FOR HITTING GOALS

What worked?

What didn't work?

What needs improving?

What are my next actions?

"Don't confuse activity with productivity. Many people are simply busy being busy."

Robin Sharma

MAY

MONDAY	TUESDAY	WEDNESDAY	THURSDAY	FRIDAY	SATURDAY	SUNDAY
☐	☐	☐	☐	☐	☐	☐

MONDAY	TUESDAY	WEDNESDAY	THURSDAY	FRIDAY	SATURDAY	SUNDAY
☐	☐	☐	☐	☐	☐	☐

MONDAY	TUESDAY	WEDNESDAY	THURSDAY	FRIDAY	SATURDAY	SUNDAY
☐	☐	☐	☐	☐	☐	☐

MONDAY	TUESDAY	WEDNESDAY	THURSDAY	FRIDAY	SATURDAY	SUNDAY
☐	☐	☐	☐	☐	☐	☐

NOTES

MONTHLY GOALS

Month:

10 Goals	The 2 most important. Why?
1.	1º
2.	
3.	
4.	
5.	Deadline:
6.	2º
7.	
8.	
9.	
10.	Deadline:

WEEK: _____	MONDAY	TUESDAY	WEDNESDAY
Goal	Goal	Goal	Goal
SECUNDARY TASKS	Priorities	Priorities	Priorities
	1...............................	1...............................	1...............................
	2...............................	2...............................	2...............................
	.3...............................	3...............................	.
	.		3...............................
	6:00...........................	6:0	6:00...........................
	7:00...........................	7:0	7:00...........................
	8:00...........................	8:0	8:00...........................
	9:00...........................	9:0	9:00...........................
	10:00.........................	10:0	10:00.........................
ADITIONAL TASKS	11:00.........................	11:0	11:00.........................
	12:00.........................	12:0	12:00.........................
	1:00...........................	1:00...........................	1:00...........................
	2:00...........................	2:00...........................	2:00...........................
	.3:00...........................	3:00...........................	3:00...........................
	4:00...........................	4:00...........................	4:00...........................
	5:00...........................	5:00...........................	5:00...........................
	6:00...........................	6:00...........................	6:00...........................
	7:00...........................	7:00...........................	7:00...........................
	8:00...........................	8:00...........................	8:00...........................
	9:00...........................	9:00...........................	9:00...........................
	10:00.........................	10:00.........................	10:00.........................
	11:00.........................	11:00.........................	11:00.........................
	12:00.........................	12:00.........................	12:00.........................

HABIT TRACKER	M	T	W	T	F	S	S

THURSDAY	FRIDAY	SATURDAY	SUNDAY
Goal	Goal	Goal	Goal
Priorities	Priorities	Priorities	Priorities
1........................	1........................	1........................	1........................
2........................	2........................	2........................	2........................
.	.	.	.
3........................	3........................	3........................	3........................
6:00...................	6:00...................	6:00...................	6:00...................
7:00...................	7:00...................	7:00...................	7:00...................
8:00...................	8:00...................	8:00...................	8:00...................
9:00...................	9:00...................	9:00...................	9:00...................
10:00.................	10:00.................	10:00.................	10:00.................
11:00.................	11:00.................	11:00.................	11:00.................
12:00.................	12:00.................	12:00.................	12:00.................
1:00...................	1:00...................	1:00...................	1:00...................
2:00...................	2:00...................	2:00...................	2:00...................
3:00...................	3:00...................	3:00...................	3:00...................
4:00...................	4:00...................	4:00...................	4:00...................
5:00...................	5:00...................	5:00...................	5:00...................
6:00...................	6:00...................	6:00...................	6:00...................
7:00...................	7:00...................	7:00...................	7:00...................
8:00...................	8:00...................	8:00...................	8:00...................
9:00...................	9:00...................	9:00...................	9:00...................
10:00.................	10:00.................	10:00.................	10:00.................
11:00.................	11:00.................	11:00.................	11:00.................
12:00	12:00.................	12:00.................	12:00.................

MILESTONES REACHED

REFLECTION ON LAST WEEK

BIGGEST WINS OF LAST WEEK	THINGS TO BE GRATEFUL FOR
IDENTIFY TIME WASTERS	...AND HOW TO REDUCE AND ELIMINATE THEM
SELF-IMPROVEMENT IDEAS	GOALS FOR THE WEEK AHEAD

REWARD FOR HITTING GOALS

What worked?

What didn't work?

What needs improving?

What are my next actions?

WEEK: _____	MONDAY	TUESDAY	WEDNESDAY
Goal	Goal	Goal	Goal
SECUNDARY TASKS	Priorities	Priorities	Priorities
	1..	1..	1..
	2..	2..	2..
	.3.......................................	3..	.
	.		3..
	6:00....................................	6:0	6:00....................................
	7:00....................................	7:0	7:00....................................
	8:00....................................	8:0	8:00....................................
	9:00....................................	9:0	9:00....................................
	10:00..................................	10:0	10:00..................................
ADITIONAL TASKS	11:00..................................	11:0	11:00..................................
	12:00..................................	12:0	12:00..................................
	1:00....................................	1:00....................................	1:00....................................
	2:00....................................	2:00....................................	2:00....................................
	.3:00...................................	3:00....................................	3:00....................................
	4:00....................................	4:00....................................	4:00....................................
	5:00....................................	5:00....................................	5:00....................................
	6:00....................................	6:00....................................	6:00....................................
	7:00....................................	7:00....................................	7:00....................................
	8:00....................................	8:00....................................	8:00....................................
	9:00....................................	9:00....................................	9:00....................................
	10:00..................................	10:00..................................	10:00..................................
	11:00..................................	11:00..................................	11:00..................................
	12:00..................................	12:00..................................	12:00..................................

HABIT TRACKER		M	T	W	T	F	S	S

THURSDAY	FRIDAY	SATURDAY	SUNDAY
Goal	Goal	Goal	Goal
Priorities	Priorities	Priorities	Priorities
1.........................	1.........................	1.........................	1.........................
2.........................	2.........................	2.........................	2.........................
.	.	.	.
3.........................	3.........................	3.........................	3.........................
6:00.....................	6:00.....................	6:00.....................	6:00.....................
7:00.....................	7:00.....................	7:00.....................	7:00.....................
8:00.....................	8:00.....................	8:00.....................	8:00.....................
9:00.....................	9:00.....................	9:00.....................	9:00.....................
10:00...................	10:00...................	10:00...................	10:00...................
11:00...................	11:00...................	11:00...................	11:00...................
12:00...................	12:00...................	12:00...................	12:00...................
1:00.....................	1:00.....................	1:00.....................	1:00.....................
2:00.....................	2:00.....................	2:00.....................	2:00.....................
3:00.....................	3:00.....................	3:00.....................	3:00.....................
4:00.....................	4:00.....................	4:00.....................	4:00.....................
5:00.....................	5:00.....................	5:00.....................	5:00.....................
6:00.....................	6:00.....................	6:00.....................	6:00.....................
7:00.....................	7:00.....................	7:00.....................	7:00.....................
8:00.....................	8:00.....................	8:00.....................	8:00.....................
9:00.....................	9:00.....................	9:00.....................	9:00.....................
10:00...................	10:00...................	10:00...................	10:00...................
11:00...................	11:00...................	11:00...................	11:00...................
12:00...................	12:00...................	12:00...................	12:00...................

MILESTONES REACHED

REFLECTION ON LAST WEEK

BIGGEST WINS OF LAST WEEK	THINGS TO BE GRATEFUL FOR
IDENTIFY TIME WASTERS	...AND HOW TO REDUCE AND ELIMINATE THEM
SELF-IMPROVEMENT IDEAS	GOALS FOR THE WEEK AHEAD

REWARD FOR HITTING GOALS

What worked?

What didn't work?

What needs improving?

What are my next actions?

WEEK: _____	MONDAY	TUESDAY	WEDNESDAY
Goal	Goal	Goal	Goal
SECUNDARY TASKS	Priorities	Priorities	Priorities

SECUNDARY TASKS	MONDAY	TUESDAY	WEDNESDAY
	1............................	1............................	1............................
	2............................	2............................	2............................
	.3............................	3............................	.
	.		3............................
	6:00........................	6:0	6:00........................
	7:00........................	7:0	7:00........................
	8:00........................	8:0	8:00........................
	9:00........................	9:0	9:00........................
	10:00.......................	10:0	10:00.......................
ADITIONAL TASKS	11:00.......................	11:0	11:00.......................
	12:00.......................	12:0	12:00.......................
	1:00........................	1:00........................	1:00........................
	2:00........................	2:00........................	2:00........................
	.3:00.......................	3:00........................	3:00........................
	4:00........................	4:00........................	4:00........................
	5:00........................	5:00........................	5:00........................
	6:00........................	6:00........................	6:00........................
	7:00........................	7:00........................	7:00........................
	8:00........................	8:00........................	8:00........................
	9:00........................	9:00........................	9:00........................
	10:00.......................	10:00.......................	10:00.......................
	11:00.......................	11:00.......................	11:00.......................
	12:00.......................	12:00.......................	12:00.......................

HABIT TRACKER				M	T	W	T	F	S	S

THURSDAY	FRIDAY	SATURDAY	SUNDAY
Goal	Goal	Goal	Goal
Priorities	Priorities	Priorities	Priorities
1.......................................	1.......................................	1.......................................	1.......................................
2.......................................	2.......................................	2.......................................	2.......................................
.	.	.	.
3.......................................	3.......................................	3.......................................	3.......................................
6:00...................................	6:00...................................	6:00...................................	6:00...................................
7:00...................................	7:00...................................	7:00...................................	7:00...................................
8:00...................................	8:00...................................	8:00...................................	8:00...................................
9:00...................................	9:00...................................	9:00...................................	9:00...................................
10:00.................................	10:00.................................	10:00.................................	10:00.................................
11:00.................................	11:00.................................	11:00.................................	11:00.................................
12:00.................................	12:00.................................	12:00.................................	12:00.................................
1:00...................................	1:00...................................	1:00...................................	1:00...................................
2:00...................................	2:00...................................	2:00...................................	2:00...................................
3:00...................................	3:00...................................	3:00...................................	3:00...................................
4:00...................................	4:00...................................	4:00...................................	4:00...................................
5:00...................................	5:00...................................	5:00...................................	5:00...................................
6:00...................................	6:00...................................	6:00...................................	6:00...................................
7:00...................................	7:00...................................	7:00...................................	7:00...................................
8:00...................................	8:00...................................	8:00...................................	8:00...................................
9:00...................................	9:00...................................	9:00...................................	9:00...................................
10:00.................................	10:00.................................	10:00.................................	10:00.................................
11:00.................................	11:00.................................	11:00.................................	11:00.................................
12:00	12:00.................................	12:00.................................	12:00.................................

MILESTONES REACHED

REFLECTION ON LAST WEEK

BIGGEST WINS OF LAST WEEK	THINGS TO BE GRATEFUL FOR
IDENTIFY TIME WASTERS	...AND HOW TO REDUCE AND ELIMINATE THEM
SELF-IMPROVEMENT IDEAS	GOALS FOR THE WEEK AHEAD

REWARD FOR HITTING GOALS

What worked?

What didn't work?

What needs improving?

What are my next actions?

WEEK: _____	MONDAY	TUESDAY	WEDNESDAY
Goal	Goal	Goal	Goal
SECUNDARY TASKS	Priorities	Priorities	Priorities
	1...............................	1...............................	1...............................
	2...............................	2...............................	2...............................
	.3...............................	3...............................	.
	.		3...............................
	6:00...............................	6:0	6:00...............................
	7:00...............................	7:0	7:00...............................
	8:00...............................	8:0	8:00...............................
	9:00...............................	9:0	9:00...............................
	10:00...............................	10:0	10:00...............................
ADITIONAL TASKS	11:00...............................	11:0	11:00...............................
	12:00...............................	12:0	12:00...............................
	1:00...............................	1:00...............................	1:00...............................
	2:00...............................	2:00...............................	2:00...............................
	.3:00...............................	3:00...............................	3:00...............................
	4:00...............................	4:00...............................	4:00...............................
	5:00...............................	5:00...............................	5:00...............................
	6:00...............................	6:00...............................	6:00...............................
	7:00...............................	7:00...............................	7:00...............................
	8:00...............................	8:00...............................	8:00...............................
	9:00...............................	9:00...............................	9:00...............................
	10:00...............................	10:00...............................	10:00...............................
	11:00...............................	11:00...............................	11:00...............................
	12:00...............................	12:00...............................	12:00...............................

HABIT TRACKER	M	T	W	T	F	S	S

THURSDAY	FRIDAY	SATURDAY	SUNDAY
Goal	Goal	Goal	Goal
Priorities	Priorities	Priorities	Priorities
1.........................	1.........................	1.........................	1.........................
2.........................	2.........................	2.........................	2.........................
.	.	.	.
3.........................	3.........................	3.........................	3.........................
6:00...................	6:00...................	6:00...................	6:00...................
7:00...................	7:00...................	7:00...................	7:00...................
8:00...................	8:00...................	8:00...................	8:00...................
9:00...................	9:00...................	9:00...................	9:00...................
10:00.................	10:00.................	10:00.................	10:00.................
11:00.................	11:00.................	11:00.................	11:00.................
12:00.................	12:00.................	12:00.................	12:00.................
1:00...................	1:00...................	1:00...................	1:00...................
2:00...................	2:00...................	2:00...................	2:00...................
3:00...................	3:00...................	3:00...................	3:00...................
4:00...................	4:00...................	4:00...................	4:00...................
5:00...................	5:00...................	5:00...................	5:00...................
6:00...................	6:00...................	6:00...................	6:00...................
7:00...................	7:00...................	7:00...................	7:00...................
8:00...................	8:00...................	8:00...................	8:00...................
9:00...................	9:00...................	9:00...................	9:00...................
10:00.................	10:00.................	10:00.................	10:00.................
11:00.................	11:00.................	11:00.................	11:00.................
12:00	12:00.................	12:00.................	12:00.................

MILESTONES REACHED

REFLECTION ON LAST WEEK

BIGGEST WINS OF LAST WEEK	THINGS TO BE GRATEFUL FOR
IDENTIFY TIME WASTERS	...AND HOW TO REDUCE AND ELIMINATE THEM
SELF-IMPROVEMENT IDEAS	GOALS FOR THE WEEK AHEAD

REWARD FOR HITTING GOALS

What worked?

What didn't work?

What needs improving?

What are my next actions?

"All you need is the plan, the road map, and the courage to press on to your destination."

Earl Nightingale

JUNE

MONTH: _____

MONDAY	TUESDAY	WEDNESDAY	THURSDAY	FRIDAY	SATURDAY	SUNDAY
☐	☐	☐	☐	☐	☐	☐
MONDAY	TUESDAY	WEDNESDAY	THURSDAY	FRIDAY	SATURDAY	SUNDAY
☐	☐	☐	☐	☐	☐	☐
MONDAY	TUESDAY	WEDNESDAY	THURSDAY	FRIDAY	SATURDAY	SUNDAY
☐	☐	☐	☐	☐	☐	☐
MONDAY	TUESDAY	WEDNESDAY	THURSDAY	FRIDAY	SATURDAY	SUNDAY
☐	☐	☐	☐	☐	☐	☐

NOTES

MONTHLY GOALS

Month:

10 Goals	The 2 most important. Why?
1.	**1º**
2.	
3.	
4.	
5.	Deadline:
6.	**2º**
7.	
8.	
9.	
10.	Deadline:

WEEK: _____	MONDAY	TUESDAY	WEDNESDAY
Goal	Goal	Goal	Goal
SECUNDARY TASKS	Priorities	Priorities	Priorities
	1.............................	1.............................	1.............................
	2.............................	2.............................	2.............................
	.3.............................	3.............................	.
	.		3.............................
	6:00.............................	6:0	6:00.............................
	7:00.............................	7:0	7:00.............................
	8:00.............................	8:0	8:00.............................
	9:00.............................	9:0	9:00.............................
	10:00.............................	10:0	10:00.............................
ADITIONAL TASKS	11:00.............................	11:0	11:00.............................
	12:00.............................	12:0	12:00.............................
	1:00.............................	1:00.............................	1:00.............................
	2:00.............................	2:00.............................	2:00.............................
	.3:00.............................	3:00.............................	3:00.............................
	4:00.............................	4:00.............................	4:00.............................
	5:00.............................	5:00.............................	5:00.............................
	6:00.............................	6:00.............................	6:00.............................
	7:00.............................	7:00.............................	7:00.............................
	8:00.............................	8:00.............................	8:00.............................
	9:00.............................	9:00.............................	9:00.............................
	10:00.............................	10:00.............................	10:00.............................
	11:00.............................	11:00.............................	11:00.............................
	12:00.............................	12:00.............................	12:00.............................

HABIT TRACKER			M	T	W	T	F	S	S

THURSDAY	FRIDAY	SATURDAY	SUNDAY
Goal	Goal	Goal	Goal
Priorities	Priorities	Priorities	Priorities
1.........................	1.........................	1.........................	1.........................
2.........................	2.........................	2.........................	2.........................
.	.	.	.
3.........................	3.........................	3.........................	3.........................
6:00.....................	6:00.....................	6:00.....................	6:00.....................
7:00.....................	7:00.....................	7:00.....................	7:00.....................
8:00.....................	8:00.....................	8:00.....................	8:00.....................
9:00.....................	9:00.....................	9:00.....................	9:00.....................
10:00....................	10:00....................	10:00....................	10:00....................
11:00....................	11:00....................	11:00....................	11:00....................
12:00....................	12:00....................	12:00....................	12:00....................
1:00.....................	1:00.....................	1:00.....................	1:00.....................
2:00.....................	2:00.....................	2:00.....................	2:00.....................
3:00.....................	3:00.....................	3:00.....................	3:00.....................
4:00.....................	4:00.....................	4:00.....................	4:00.....................
5:00.....................	5:00.....................	5:00.....................	5:00.....................
6:00.....................	6:00.....................	6:00.....................	6:00.....................
7:00.....................	7:00.....................	7:00.....................	7:00.....................
8:00.....................	8:00.....................	8:00.....................	8:00.....................
9:00.....................	9:00.....................	9:00.....................	9:00.....................
10:00....................	10:00....................	10:00....................	10:00....................
11:00....................	11:00....................	11:00....................	11:00....................
12:00	12:00....................	12:00....................	12:00....................

MILESTONES REACHED

REFLECTION ON LAST WEEK

BIGGEST WINS OF LAST WEEK	THINGS TO BE GRATEFUL FOR
IDENTIFY TIME WASTERS	...AND HOW TO REDUCE AND ELIMINATE THEM
SELF-IMPROVEMENT IDEAS	GOALS FOR THE WEEK AHEAD

REWARD FOR HITTING GOALS

What worked?

What didn't work?

What needs improving?

What are my next actions?

WEEK: _____	MONDAY	TUESDAY	WEDNESDAY
Goal	Goal	Goal	Goal
SECUNDARY TASKS	Priorities	Priorities	Priorities
	1.............................	1.............................	1.............................
	2.............................	2.............................	2.............................
	3.............................	3.............................	.
	.		3.............................
	6:00.........................	6:0	6:00.........................
	7:00.........................	7:0	7:00.........................
	8:00.........................	8:0	8:00.........................
	9:00.........................	9:0	9:00.........................
	10:00.......................	10:0	10:00.......................
ADITIONAL TASKS	11:00.......................	11:0	11:00.......................
	12:00.......................	12:0	12:00.......................
	1:00.........................	1:00.........................	1:00.........................
	2:00.........................	2:00.........................	2:00.........................
	3:00.........................	3:00.........................	3:00.........................
	4:00.........................	4:00.........................	4:00.........................
	5:00.........................	5:00.........................	5:00.........................
	6:00.........................	6:00.........................	6:00.........................
	7:00.........................	7:00.........................	7:00.........................
	8:00.........................	8:00.........................	8:00.........................
	9:00.........................	9:00.........................	9:00.........................
	10:00.......................	10:00.......................	10:00.......................
	11:00.......................	11:00.......................	11:00.......................
	12:00.......................	12:00.......................	12:00.......................

HABIT TRACKER			M	T	W	T	F	S	S

THURSDAY	FRIDAY	SATURDAY	SUNDAY
Goal	Goal	Goal	Goal
Priorities	Priorities	Priorities	Priorities
1.........................	1.........................	1.........................	1.........................
2.........................	2.........................	2.........................	2.........................
.	.	.	.
3.........................	3.........................	3.........................	3.........................
6:00.....................	6:00.....................	6:00.....................	6:00.....................
7:00.....................	7:00.....................	7:00.....................	7:00.....................
8:00.....................	8:00.....................	8:00.....................	8:00.....................
9:00.....................	9:00.....................	9:00.....................	9:00.....................
10:00....................	10:00....................	10:00....................	10:00....................
11:00....................	11:00....................	11:00....................	11:00....................
12:00....................	12:00....................	12:00....................	12:00....................
1:00.....................	1:00.....................	1:00.....................	1:00.....................
2:00.....................	2:00.....................	2:00.....................	2:00.....................
3:00.....................	3:00.....................	3:00.....................	3:00.....................
4:00.....................	4:00.....................	4:00.....................	4:00.....................
5:00.....................	5:00.....................	5:00.....................	5:00.....................
6:00.....................	6:00.....................	6:00.....................	6:00.....................
7:00.....................	7:00.....................	7:00.....................	7:00.....................
8:00.....................	8:00.....................	8:00.....................	8:00.....................
9:00.....................	9:00.....................	9:00.....................	9:00.....................
10:00....................	10:00....................	10:00....................	10:00....................
11:00....................	11:00....................	11:00....................	11:00....................
12:00	12:00....................	12:00....................	12:00....................

MILESTONES REACHED

REFLECTION ON LAST WEEK

BIGGEST WINS OF LAST WEEK	THINGS TO BE GRATEFUL FOR
IDENTIFY TIME WASTERS	...AND HOW TO REDUCE AND ELIMINATE THEM
SELF-IMPROVEMENT IDEAS	GOALS FOR THE WEEK AHEAD

REWARD FOR HITTING GOALS

What worked?

What didn't work?

What needs improving?

What are my next actions?

WEEK: _____	MONDAY	TUESDAY	WEDNESDAY
Goal	Goal	Goal	Goal
SECUNDARY TASKS	Priorities	Priorities	Priorities
	1..........................	1..........................	1..........................
	2..........................	2..........................	2..........................
	.3..........................	3..........................	.
	.		3..........................
	6:00..........................	6:0	6:00..........................
	7:00..........................	7:0	7:00..........................
	8:00..........................	8:0	8:00..........................
	9:00..........................	9:0	9:00..........................
	10:00..........................	10:0	10:00..........................
ADITIONAL TASKS	11:00..........................	11:0	11:00..........................
	12:00..........................	12:0	12:00..........................
	1:00..........................	1:00..........................	1:00..........................
	2:00..........................	2:00..........................	2:00..........................
	.3:00..........................	3:00..........................	3:00..........................
	4:00..........................	4:00..........................	4:00..........................
	5:00..........................	5:00..........................	5:00..........................
	6:00..........................	6:00..........................	6:00..........................
	7:00..........................	7:00..........................	7:00..........................
	8:00..........................	8:00..........................	8:00..........................
	9:00..........................	9:00..........................	9:00..........................
	10:00..........................	10:00..........................	10:00..........................
	11:00..........................	11:00..........................	11:00..........................
	12:00..........................	12:00..........................	12:00..........................

HABIT TRACKER	M	T	W	T	F	S	S

THURSDAY	FRIDAY	SATURDAY	SUNDAY
Goal	Goal	Goal	Goal
Priorities	Priorities	Priorities	Priorities
1.........................	1.........................	1.........................	1.........................
2.........................	2.........................	2.........................	2.........................
.	.	.	.
3.........................	3.........................	3.........................	3.........................
6:00..................	6:00..................	6:00..................	6:00..................
7:00..................	7:00..................	7:00..................	7:00..................
8:00..................	8:00..................	8:00..................	8:00..................
9:00..................	9:00..................	9:00..................	9:00..................
10:00................	10:00................	10:00................	10:00................
11:00................	11:00................	11:00................	11:00................
12:00................	12:00................	12:00................	12:00................
1:00..................	1:00..................	1:00..................	1:00..................
2:00..................	2:00..................	2:00..................	2:00..................
3:00..................	3:00..................	3:00..................	3:00..................
4:00..................	4:00..................	4:00..................	4:00..................
5:00..................	5:00..................	5:00..................	5:00..................
6:00..................	6:00..................	6:00..................	6:00..................
7:00..................	7:00..................	7:00..................	7:00..................
8:00..................	8:00..................	8:00..................	8:00..................
9:00..................	9:00..................	9:00..................	9:00..................
10:00................	10:00................	10:00................	10:00................
11:00................	11:00................	11:00................	11:00................
12:00................	12:00................	12:00................	12:00................
MILESTONES REACHED			

REFLECTION ON LAST WEEK

BIGGEST WINS OF LAST WEEK	THINGS TO BE GRATEFUL FOR
IDENTIFY TIME WASTERS	...AND HOW TO REDUCE AND ELIMINATE THEM
SELF-IMPROVEMENT IDEAS	GOALS FOR THE WEEK AHEAD

REWARD FOR HITTING GOALS

What worked?

What didn't work?

What needs improving?

What are my next actions?

WEEK: _____	MONDAY	TUESDAY	WEDNESDAY
Goal	Goal	Goal	Goal
SECUNDARY TASKS	Priorities	Priorities	Priorities
	1...	1...	1...
	2...	2...	2...
	.3...	3...	.
	.		3...
	6:00...	6:0	6:00...
	7:00...	7:0	7:00...
	8:00...	8:0	8:00...
	9:00...	9:0	9:00...
	10:00...	10:0	10:00...
ADITIONAL TASKS	11:00...	11:0	11:00...
	12:00...	12:0	12:00...
	1:00...	1:00...	1:00...
	2:00...	2:00...	2:00...
	.3:00...	3:00...	3:00...
	4:00...	4:00...	4:00...
	5:00...	5:00...	5:00...
	6:00...	6:00...	6:00...
	7:00...	7:00...	7:00...
	8:00...	8:00...	8:00...
	9:00...	9:00...	9:00...
	10:00...	10:00...	10:00...
	11:00...	11:00...	11:00...
	12:00...	12:00...	12:00...

HABIT TRACKER				M	T	W	T	F	S	S

THURSDAY	FRIDAY	SATURDAY	SUNDAY
Goal	Goal	Goal	Goal
Priorities	Priorities	Priorities	Priorities
1...	1...	1...	1...
2...	2...	2...	2...
.	.	.	.
3...	3...	3...	3...
6:00...	6:00...	6:00...	6:00...
7:00...	7:00...	7:00...	7:00...
8:00...	8:00...	8:00...	8:00...
9:00...	9:00...	9:00...	9:00...
10:00...	10:00...	10:00...	10:00...
11:00...	11:00...	11:00...	11:00...
12:00...	12:00...	12:00...	12:00...
1:00...	1:00...	1:00...	1:00...
2:00...	2:00...	2:00...	2:00...
3:00...	3:00...	3:00...	3:00...
4:00...	4:00...	4:00...	4:00...
5:00...	5:00...	5:00...	5:00...
6:00...	6:00...	6:00...	6:00...
7:00...	7:00...	7:00...	7:00...
8:00...	8:00...	8:00...	8:00...
9:00...	9:00...	9:00...	9:00...
10:00...	10:00...	10:00...	10:00...
11:00...	11:00...	11:00...	11:00...
12:00...	12:00...	12:00...	12:00...

MILESTONES REACHED

REFLECTION ON LAST WEEK

BIGGEST WINS OF LAST WEEK	THINGS TO BE GRATEFUL FOR
IDENTIFY TIME WASTERS	...AND HOW TO REDUCE AND ELIMINATE THEM
SELF-IMPROVEMENT IDEAS	GOALS FOR THE WEEK AHEAD

REWARD FOR HITTING GOALS

What worked?

What didn't work?

What needs improving?

What are my next actions?

END OF
SEMESTER
REFLECTION

What were the three biggest lessons you've learned this past semester?

Review your planner for this past semester and assess your priorities. Are you happy with how you spent your time? If not, what steps can you take for the next semester to adjust them?

What did you accomplish this past semester? What are you most proud of?

Name three things you can improve on the next semester. What concrete actions can you take to work towards these improvements?

What or who are you especially grateful for this past semester?

"Determine that the thing can and shall be done, and then we shall find the way."

Abraham Lincoln

JULY

MONDAY	TUESDAY	WEDNESDAY	THURSDAY	FRIDAY	SATURDAY	SUNDAY
☐	☐	☐	☐	☐	☐	☐

MONDAY	TUESDAY	WEDNESDAY	THURSDAY	FRIDAY	SATURDAY	SUNDAY
☐	☐	☐	☐	☐	☐	☐

MONDAY	TUESDAY	WEDNESDAY	THURSDAY	FRIDAY	SATURDAY	SUNDAY
☐	☐	☐	☐	☐	☐	☐

MONDAY	TUESDAY	WEDNESDAY	THURSDAY	FRIDAY	SATURDAY	SUNDAY
☐	☐	☐	☐	☐	☐	☐

NOTES

MONTHLY GOALS

Month:

10 Goals	The 2 most important. Why?
1.	**1º**
2.	
3.	
4.	
5.	Deadline:
6.	**2º**
7.	
8.	
9.	
10.	Deadline:

WEEK: _____	MONDAY	TUESDAY	WEDNESDAY
Goal	Goal	Goal	Goal
SECUNDARY TASKS	Priorities	Priorities	Priorities
	1..............................	1..............................	1..............................
	2..............................	2..............................	2..............................
	3..............................	3..............................	.
	.		3..............................
	6:00..........................	6:0	6:00..........................
	7:00..........................	7:0	7:00..........................
	8:00..........................	8:0	8:00..........................
	9:00..........................	9:0	9:00..........................
	10:00........................	10:0	10:00........................
ADITIONAL TASKS	11:00........................	11:0	11:00........................
	12:00........................	12:0	12:00........................
	1:00..........................	1:00..........................	1:00..........................
	2:00..........................	2:00..........................	2:00..........................
	3:00..........................	3:00..........................	3:00..........................
	4:00..........................	4:00..........................	4:00..........................
	5:00..........................	5:00..........................	5:00..........................
	6:00..........................	6:00..........................	6:00..........................
	7:00..........................	7:00..........................	7:00..........................
	8:00..........................	8:00..........................	8:00..........................
	9:00..........................	9:00..........................	9:00..........................
	10:00........................	10:00........................	10:00........................
	11:00........................	11:00........................	11:00........................
	12:00........................	12:00........................	12:00........................

HABIT TRACKER			M	T	W	T	F	S	S

THURSDAY	FRIDAY	SATURDAY	SUNDAY
Goal	Goal	Goal	Goal
Priorities	Priorities	Priorities	Priorities
1..........................	1..........................	1..........................	1..........................
2..........................	2..........................	2..........................	2..........................
.	.	.	.
3..........................	3..........................	3..........................	3..........................
6:00..........................	6:00..........................	6:00..........................	6:00..........................
7:00..........................	7:00..........................	7:00..........................	7:00..........................
8:00..........................	8:00..........................	8:00..........................	8:00..........................
9:00..........................	9:00..........................	9:00..........................	9:00..........................
10:00..........................	10:00..........................	10:00..........................	10:00..........................
11:00..........................	11:00..........................	11:00..........................	11:00..........................
12:00..........................	12:00..........................	12:00..........................	12:00..........................
1:00..........................	1:00..........................	1:00..........................	1:00..........................
2:00..........................	2:00..........................	2:00..........................	2:00..........................
3:00..........................	3:00..........................	3:00..........................	3:00..........................
4:00..........................	4:00..........................	4:00..........................	4:00..........................
5:00..........................	5:00..........................	5:00..........................	5:00..........................
6:00..........................	6:00..........................	6:00..........................	6:00..........................
7:00..........................	7:00..........................	7:00..........................	7:00..........................
8:00..........................	8:00..........................	8:00..........................	8:00..........................
9:00..........................	9:00..........................	9:00..........................	9:00..........................
10:00..........................	10:00..........................	10:00..........................	10:00..........................
11:00..........................	11:00..........................	11:00..........................	11:00..........................
12:00..........................	12:00..........................	12:00..........................	12:00..........................

MILESTONES REACHED

REFLECTION ON LAST WEEK

BIGGEST WINS OF LAST WEEK	THINGS TO BE GRATEFUL FOR
IDENTIFY TIME WASTERS	...AND HOW TO REDUCE AND ELIMINATE THEM
SELF-IMPROVEMENT IDEAS	GOALS FOR THE WEEK AHEAD

REWARD FOR HITTING GOALS

What worked?

What didn't work?

What needs improving?

What are my next actions?

WEEK: _____	MONDAY	TUESDAY	WEDNESDAY
Goal	Goal	Goal	Goal
SECUNDARY TASKS	Priorities	Priorities	Priorities
	1...............................	1...............................	1...............................
	2...............................	2...............................	2...............................
	.3...............................	3...............................	.
	.		3...............................
	6:00...............................	6:0	6:00...............................
	7:00...............................	7:0	7:00...............................
	8:00...............................	8:0	8:00...............................
	9:00...............................	9:0	9:00...............................
	10:00...............................	10:0	10:00...............................
ADITIONAL TASKS	11:00...............................	11:0	11:00...............................
	12:00...............................	12:0	12:00...............................
	1:00...............................	1:00...............................	1:00...............................
	2:00...............................	2:00...............................	2:00...............................
	.3:00...............................	3:00...............................	3:00...............................
	4:00...............................	4:00...............................	4:00...............................
	5:00...............................	5:00...............................	5:00...............................
	6:00...............................	6:00...............................	6:00...............................
	7:00...............................	7:00...............................	7:00...............................
	8:00...............................	8:00...............................	8:00...............................
	9:00...............................	9:00...............................	9:00...............................
	10:00...............................	10:00...............................	10:00...............................
	11:00...............................	11:00...............................	11:00...............................
	12:00...............................	12:00...............................	12:00...............................

HABIT TRACKER	M	T	W	T	F	S	S

THURSDAY	FRIDAY	SATURDAY	SUNDAY
Goal	Goal	Goal	Goal
Priorities	Priorities	Priorities	Priorities
1...	1...	1...	1...
2...	2...	2...	2...
.	.	.	.
3...	3...	3...	3...
6:00...	6:00...	6:00...	6:00...
7:00...	7:00...	7:00...	7:00...
8:00...	8:00...	8:00...	8:00...
9:00...	9:00...	9:00...	9:00...
10:00...	10:00...	10:00...	10:00...
11:00...	11:00...	11:00...	11:00...
12:00...	12:00...	12:00...	12:00...
1:00...	1:00...	1:00...	1:00...
2:00...	2:00...	2:00...	2:00...
3:00...	3:00...	3:00...	3:00...
4:00...	4:00...	4:00...	4:00...
5:00...	5:00...	5:00...	5:00...
6:00...	6:00...	6:00...	6:00...
7:00...	7:00...	7:00...	7:00...
8:00...	8:00...	8:00...	8:00...
9:00...	9:00...	9:00...	9:00...
10:00...	10:00...	10:00...	10:00...
11:00...	11:00...	11:00...	11:00...
12:00	12:00...	12:00...	12:00...

MILESTONES REACHED

REFLECTION ON LAST WEEK

BIGGEST WINS OF LAST WEEK	THINGS TO BE GRATEFUL FOR
IDENTIFY TIME WASTERS	...AND HOW TO REDUCE AND ELIMINATE THEM
SELF-IMPROVEMENT IDEAS	GOALS FOR THE WEEK AHEAD

REWARD FOR HITTING GOALS

What worked?

What didn't work?

What needs improving?

What are my next actions?

WEEK: _____	MONDAY	TUESDAY	WEDNESDAY
Goal	Goal	Goal	Goal
SECUNDARY TASKS	Priorities	Priorities	Priorities

SECUNDARY TASKS	Priorities	Priorities	Priorities
	1................................	1................................	1................................
	2................................	2................................	2................................
	.3................................	3................................	.
	.		3................................
	6:00............................	6:0	6:00............................
	7:00............................	7:0	7:00............................
	8:00............................	8:0	8:00............................
	9:00............................	9:0	9:00............................
	10:00............................	10:0	10:00............................
ADITIONAL TASKS	11:00............................	11:0	11:00............................
	12:00............................	12:0	12:00............................
	1:00............................	1:00............................	1:00............................
	2:00............................	2:00............................	2:00............................
	.3:00............................	3:00............................	3:00............................
	4:00............................	4:00............................	4:00............................
	5:00............................	5:00............................	5:00............................
	6:00............................	6:00............................	6:00............................
	7:00............................	7:00............................	7:00............................
	8:00............................	8:00............................	8:00............................
	9:00............................	9:00............................	9:00............................
	10:00............................	10:00............................	10:00............................
	11:00............................	11:00............................	11:00............................
	12:00............................	12:00............................	12:00............................

HABIT TRACKER			M	T	W	T	F	S	S

THURSDAY	FRIDAY	SATURDAY	SUNDAY
Goal	Goal	Goal	Goal
Priorities	Priorities	Priorities	Priorities
1...................................... 2...................................... . 3......................................	1...................................... 2...................................... . 3......................................	1...................................... 2...................................... . 3......................................	1...................................... 2...................................... . 3......................................
6:00..................................	6:00..................................	6:00..................................	6:00..................................
7:00..................................	7:00..................................	7:00..................................	7:00..................................
8:00..................................	8:00..................................	8:00..................................	8:00..................................
9:00..................................	9:00..................................	9:00..................................	9:00..................................
10:00................................	10:00................................	10:00................................	10:00................................
11:00................................	11:00................................	11:00................................	11:00................................
12:00................................	12:00................................	12:00................................	12:00................................
1:00..................................	1:00..................................	1:00..................................	1:00..................................
2:00..................................	2:00..................................	2:00..................................	2:00..................................
3:00..................................	3:00..................................	3:00..................................	3:00..................................
4:00..................................	4:00..................................	4:00..................................	4:00..................................
5:00..................................	5:00..................................	5:00..................................	5:00..................................
6:00..................................	6:00..................................	6:00..................................	6:00..................................
7:00..................................	7:00..................................	7:00..................................	7:00..................................
8:00..................................	8:00..................................	8:00..................................	8:00..................................
9:00..................................	9:00..................................	9:00..................................	9:00..................................
10:00................................	10:00................................	10:00................................	10:00................................
11:00................................	11:00................................	11:00................................	11:00................................
12:00	12:00................................	12:00................................	12:00................................

MILESTONES REACHED

REFLECTION ON LAST WEEK

BIGGEST WINS OF LAST WEEK	THINGS TO BE GRATEFUL FOR
IDENTIFY TIME WASTERS	...AND HOW TO REDUCE AND ELIMINATE THEM
SELF-IMPROVEMENT IDEAS	GOALS FOR THE WEEK AHEAD

REWARD FOR HITTING GOALS

What worked?

What didn't work?

What needs improving?

What are my next actions?

WEEK: _____	MONDAY	TUESDAY	WEDNESDAY
Goal	**Goal**	**Goal**	**Goal**
SECUNDARY TASKS	**Priorities**	**Priorities**	**Priorities**
	1..............................	1..............................	1..............................
	2..............................	2..............................	2..............................
	3..............................	3..............................	.
	.		3..............................
	6:00..........................	6:0	6:00..........................
	7:00..........................	7:0	7:00..........................
	8:00..........................	8:0	8:00..........................
	9:00..........................	9:0	9:00..........................
	10:00.........................	10:0	10:00.........................
ADITIONAL TASKS	11:00.........................	11:0	11:00.........................
	12:00.........................	12:0	12:00.........................
	1:00..........................	1:00..........................	1:00..........................
	2:00..........................	2:00..........................	2:00..........................
	3:00..........................	3:00..........................	3:00..........................
	4:00..........................	4:00..........................	4:00..........................
	5:00..........................	5:00..........................	5:00..........................
	6:00..........................	6:00..........................	6:00..........................
	7:00..........................	7:00..........................	7:00..........................
	8:00..........................	8:00..........................	8:00..........................
	9:00..........................	9:00..........................	9:00..........................
	10:00.........................	10:00.........................	10:00.........................
	11:00.........................	11:00.........................	11:00.........................
	12:00.........................	12:00.........................	12:00.........................

HABIT TRACKER	M	T	W	T	F	S	S

THURSDAY	FRIDAY	SATURDAY	SUNDAY
Goal	Goal	Goal	Goal
Priorities	Priorities	Priorities	Priorities
1..	1..	1..	1..
2..	2..	2..	2..
.	.	.	.
3..	3..	3..	3..
6:00..	6:00..	6:00..	6:00..
7:00..	7:00..	7:00..	7:00..
8:00..	8:00..	8:00..	8:00..
9:00..	9:00..	9:00..	9:00..
10:00..	10:00..	10:00..	10:00..
11:00..	11:00..	11:00..	11:00..
12:00..	12:00..	12:00..	12:00..
1:00..	1:00..	1:00..	1:00..
2:00..	2:00..	2:00..	2:00..
3:00..	3:00..	3:00..	3:00..
4:00..	4:00..	4:00..	4:00..
5:00..	5:00..	5:00..	5:00..
6:00..	6:00..	6:00..	6:00..
7:00..	7:00..	7:00..	7:00..
8:00..	8:00..	8:00..	8:00..
9:00..	9:00..	9:00..	9:00..
10:00..	10:00..	10:00..	10:00..
11:00..	11:00..	11:00..	11:00..
12:00	12:00..	12:00..	12:00..

MILESTONES REACHED

REFLECTION ON LAST WEEK

BIGGEST WINS OF LAST WEEK	THINGS TO BE GRATEFUL FOR
IDENTIFY TIME WASTERS	...AND HOW TO REDUCE AND ELIMINATE THEM
SELF-IMPROVEMENT IDEAS	GOALS FOR THE WEEK AHEAD

REWARD FOR HITTING GOALS

What worked?

What didn't work?

What needs improving?

What are my next actions?

"The secret of getting ahead is getting started".

Mark Twain

AUGUST

MONDAY	TUESDAY	WEDNESDAY	THURSDAY	FRIDAY	SATURDAY	SUNDAY
☐	☐	☐	☐	☐	☐	☐

MONDAY	TUESDAY	WEDNESDAY	THURSDAY	FRIDAY	SATURDAY	SUNDAY
☐	☐	☐	☐	☐	☐	☐

MONDAY	TUESDAY	WEDNESDAY	THURSDAY	FRIDAY	SATURDAY	SUNDAY
☐	☐	☐	☐	☐	☐	☐

MONDAY	TUESDAY	WEDNESDAY	THURSDAY	FRIDAY	SATURDAY	SUNDAY
☐	☐	☐	☐	☐	☐	☐

NOTES

MONTHLY GOALS

Month:

10 Goals	The 2 most important. Why?
1.	**1º**
2.	
3.	
4.	
5.	Deadline:
6.	**2º**
7.	
8.	
9.	
10.	Deadline:

WEEK: _____	MONDAY	TUESDAY	WEDNESDAY
Goal	Goal	Goal	Goal
SECUNDARY TASKS	Priorities	Priorities	Priorities
	1............................	1............................	1............................
	2............................	2............................	2............................
	.3............................	3............................	.
	.		3............................
	6:00............................	6:0	6:00............................
	7:00............................	7:0	7:00............................
	8:00............................	8:0	8:00............................
	9:00............................	9:0	9:00............................
	10:00............................	10:0	10:00............................
ADITIONAL TASKS	11:00............................	11:0	11:00............................
	12:00............................	12:0	12:00............................
	1:00............................	1:00............................	1:00............................
	2:00............................	2:00............................	2:00............................
	.3:00............................	3:00............................	3:00............................
	4:00............................	4:00............................	4:00............................
	5:00............................	5:00............................	5:00............................
	6:00............................	6:00............................	6:00............................
	7:00............................	7:00............................	7:00............................
	8:00............................	8:00............................	8:00............................
	9:00............................	9:00............................	9:00............................
	10:00............................	10:00............................	10:00............................
	11:00............................	11:00............................	11:00............................
	12:00............................	12:00............................	12:00............................

HABIT TRACKER	M	T	W	T	F	S	S

THURSDAY	FRIDAY	SATURDAY	SUNDAY
Goal	Goal	Goal	Goal
Priorities	Priorities	Priorities	Priorities
1.........................	1.........................	1.........................	1.........................
2.........................	2.........................	2.........................	2.........................
.	.	.	.
3.........................	3.........................	3.........................	3.........................
6:00.....................	6:00.....................	6:00.....................	6:00.....................
7:00.....................	7:00.....................	7:00.....................	7:00.....................
8:00.....................	8:00.....................	8:00.....................	8:00.....................
9:00.....................	9:00.....................	9:00.....................	9:00.....................
10:00...................	10:00...................	10:00...................	10:00...................
11:00...................	11:00...................	11:00...................	11:00...................
12:00...................	12:00...................	12:00...................	12:00...................
1:00.....................	1:00.....................	1:00.....................	1:00.....................
2:00.....................	2:00.....................	2:00.....................	2:00.....................
3:00.....................	3:00.....................	3:00.....................	3:00.....................
4:00.....................	4:00.....................	4:00.....................	4:00.....................
5:00.....................	5:00.....................	5:00.....................	5:00.....................
6:00.....................	6:00.....................	6:00.....................	6:00.....................
7:00.....................	7:00.....................	7:00.....................	7:00.....................
8:00.....................	8:00.....................	8:00.....................	8:00.....................
9:00.....................	9:00.....................	9:00.....................	9:00.....................
10:00...................	10:00...................	10:00...................	10:00...................
11:00...................	11:00...................	11:00...................	11:00...................
12:00	12:00	12:00	12:00 ....

MILESTONES REACHED

REFLECTION ON LAST WEEK

BIGGEST WINS OF LAST WEEK	THINGS TO BE GRATEFUL FOR
IDENTIFY TIME WASTERS	...AND HOW TO REDUCE AND ELIMINATE THEM
SELF-IMPROVEMENT IDEAS	GOALS FOR THE WEEK AHEAD

REWARD FOR HITTING GOALS

What worked?

What didn't work?

What needs improving?

What are my next actions?

WEEK: _____	MONDAY	TUESDAY	WEDNESDAY
Goal	Goal	Goal	Goal
SECUNDARY TASKS	Priorities	Priorities	Priorities
	1................................	1................................	1................................
	2................................	2................................	2................................
	3................................	3................................	.
	.		3................................
	6:00..........................	6:0	6:00..........................
	7:00..........................	7:0	7:00..........................
	8:00..........................	8:0	8:00..........................
	9:00..........................	9:0	9:00..........................
	10:00........................	10:0	10:00........................
ADITIONAL TASKS	11:00........................	11:0	11:00........................
	12:00........................	12:0	12:00........................
	1:00..........................	1:00.........................	1:00..........................
	2:00..........................	2:00.........................	2:00..........................
	.3:00.........................	3:00.........................	3:00..........................
	4:00..........................	4:00.........................	4:00..........................
	5:00..........................	5:00.........................	5:00..........................
	6:00..........................	6:00.........................	6:00..........................
	7:00..........................	7:00.........................	7:00..........................
	8:00..........................	8:00.........................	8:00..........................
	9:00..........................	9:00.........................	9:00..........................
	10:00........................	10:00.......................	10:00........................
	11:00........................	11:00.......................	11:00........................
	12:00........................	12:00.......................	12:00........................

HABIT TRACKER			M	T	W	T	F	S	S

THURSDAY	FRIDAY	SATURDAY	SUNDAY
Goal	Goal	Goal	Goal
Priorities	Priorities	Priorities	Priorities
1..............................	1..............................	1..............................	1..............................
2..............................	2..............................	2..............................	2..............................
.	.	.	.
3..............................	3..............................	3..............................	3..............................
6:00..........................	6:00..........................	6:00..........................	6:00..........................
7:00..........................	7:00..........................	7:00..........................	7:00..........................
8:00..........................	8:00..........................	8:00..........................	8:00..........................
9:00..........................	9:00..........................	9:00..........................	9:00..........................
10:00........................	10:00........................	10:00........................	10:00........................
11:00........................	11:00........................	11:00........................	11:00........................
12:00........................	12:00........................	12:00........................	12:00........................
1:00..........................	1:00..........................	1:00..........................	1:00..........................
2:00..........................	2:00..........................	2:00..........................	2:00..........................
3:00..........................	3:00..........................	3:00..........................	3:00..........................
4:00..........................	4:00..........................	4:00..........................	4:00..........................
5:00..........................	5:00..........................	5:00..........................	5:00..........................
6:00..........................	6:00..........................	6:00..........................	6:00..........................
7:00..........................	7:00..........................	7:00..........................	7:00..........................
8:00..........................	8:00..........................	8:00..........................	8:00..........................
9:00..........................	9:00..........................	9:00..........................	9:00..........................
10:00........................	10:00........................	10:00........................	10:00........................
11:00........................	11:00........................	11:00........................	11:00........................
12:00	12:00........................	12:00........................	12:00........................

MILESTONES REACHED

REFLECTION ON LAST WEEK

BIGGEST WINS OF LAST WEEK	THINGS TO BE GRATEFUL FOR
IDENTIFY TIME WASTERS	...AND HOW TO REDUCE AND ELIMINATE THEM
SELF-IMPROVEMENT IDEAS	GOALS FOR THE WEEK AHEAD

REWARD FOR HITTING GOALS

What worked?

What didn't work?

What needs improving?

What are my next actions?

WEEK: _____	MONDAY	TUESDAY	WEDNESDAY
Goal	Goal	Goal	Goal
SECUNDARY TASKS	Priorities	Priorities	Priorities
	1.............................	1.............................	1.............................
	2.............................	2.............................	2.............................
	.3............................	3............................	.
	.		3............................
	6:00.......................	6:0	6:00.......................
	7:00.......................	7:0	7:00.......................
	8:00.......................	8:0	8:00.......................
	9:00.......................	9:0	9:00.......................
	10:00.....................	10:0	10:00.....................
ADITIONAL TASKS	11:00.....................	11:0	11:00.....................
	12:00.....................	12:0	12:00.....................
	1:00.......................	1:00.......................	1:00.......................
	2:00.......................	2:00.......................	2:00.......................
	.3:00......................	3:00.......................	3:00.......................
	4:00.......................	4:00.......................	4:00.......................
	5:00.......................	5:00.......................	5:00.......................
	6:00.......................	6:00.......................	6:00.......................
	7:00.......................	7:00.......................	7:00.......................
	8:00.......................	8:00.......................	8:00.......................
	9:00.......................	9:00.......................	9:00.......................
	10:00.....................	10:00.....................	10:00.....................
	11:00.....................	11:00.....................	11:00.....................
	12:00.....................	12:00.....................	12:00.....................

HABIT TRACKER	M	T	W	T	F	S	S

THURSDAY	FRIDAY	SATURDAY	SUNDAY
Goal	Goal	Goal	Goal
Priorities	Priorities	Priorities	Priorities
1...............................	1...............................	1...............................	1...............................
2...............................	2...............................	2...............................	2...............................
.	.	.	.
3...............................	3...............................	3...............................	3...............................
6:00............................	6:00............................	6:00............................	6:00............................
7:00............................	7:00............................	7:00............................	7:00............................
8:00............................	8:00............................	8:00............................	8:00............................
9:00............................	9:00............................	9:00............................	9:00............................
10:00..........................	10:00..........................	10:00..........................	10:00..........................
11:00..........................	11:00..........................	11:00..........................	11:00..........................
12:00..........................	12:00..........................	12:00..........................	12:00..........................
1:00............................	1:00............................	1:00............................	1:00............................
2:00............................	2:00............................	2:00............................	2:00............................
3:00............................	3:00............................	3:00............................	3:00............................
4:00............................	4:00............................	4:00............................	4:00............................
5:00............................	5:00............................	5:00............................	5:00............................
6:00............................	6:00............................	6:00............................	6:00............................
7:00............................	7:00............................	7:00............................	7:00............................
8:00............................	8:00............................	8:00............................	8:00............................
9:00............................	9:00............................	9:00............................	9:00............................
10:00..........................	10:00..........................	10:00..........................	10:00..........................
11:00..........................	11:00..........................	11:00..........................	11:00..........................
12:00	12:00..........................	12:00..........................	12:00..........................

MILESTONES REACHED

REFLECTION ON LAST WEEK

BIGGEST WINS OF LAST WEEK	THINGS TO BE GRATEFUL FOR
IDENTIFY TIME WASTERS	...AND HOW TO REDUCE AND ELIMINATE THEM
SELF-IMPROVEMENT IDEAS	GOALS FOR THE WEEK AHEAD

REWARD FOR HITTING GOALS

What worked?

What didn't work?

What needs improving?

What are my next actions?

WEEK: _____	MONDAY	TUESDAY	WEDNESDAY
Goal	Goal	Goal	Goal
SECUNDARY TASKS	Priorities	Priorities	Priorities
	1...	1...	1...
	2...	2...	2...
	3...	3...	.
	.		3...
	6:00.....................................	6:0	6:00.....................................
	7:00.....................................	7:0	7:00.....................................
	8:00.....................................	8:0	8:00.....................................
	9:00.....................................	9:0	9:00.....................................
	10:00...................................	10:0	10:00...................................
ADITIONAL TASKS	11:00...................................	11:0	11:00...................................
	12:00...................................	12:0	12:00...................................
	1:00.....................................	1:00.....................................	1:00.....................................
	2:00.....................................	2:00.....................................	2:00.....................................
	3:00.....................................	3:00.....................................	3:00.....................................
	4:00.....................................	4:00.....................................	4:00.....................................
	5:00.....................................	5:00.....................................	5:00.....................................
	6:00.....................................	6:00.....................................	6:00.....................................
	7:00.....................................	7:00.....................................	7:00.....................................
	8:00.....................................	8:00.....................................	8:00.....................................
	9:00.....................................	9:00.....................................	9:00.....................................
	10:00...................................	10:00...................................	10:00...................................
	11:00...................................	11:00...................................	11:00...................................
	12:00...................................	12:00...................................	12:00...................................

HABIT TRACKER			M	T	W	T	F	S	S

THURSDAY	FRIDAY	SATURDAY	SUNDAY
Goal	Goal	Goal	Goal
Priorities	Priorities	Priorities	Priorities
1............................	1............................	1............................	1............................
2............................	2............................	2............................	2............................
.	.	.	.
3............................	3............................	3............................	3............................
6:00........................	6:00........................	6:00........................	6:00........................
7:00........................	7:00........................	7:00........................	7:00........................
8:00........................	8:00........................	8:00........................	8:00........................
9:00........................	9:00........................	9:00........................	9:00........................
10:00......................	10:00......................	10:00......................	10:00......................
11:00......................	11:00......................	11:00......................	11:00......................
12:00......................	12:00......................	12:00......................	12:00......................
1:00........................	1:00........................	1:00........................	1:00........................
2:00........................	2:00........................	2:00........................	2:00........................
3:00........................	3:00........................	3:00........................	3:00........................
4:00........................	4:00........................	4:00........................	4:00........................
5:00........................	5:00........................	5:00........................	5:00........................
6:00........................	6:00........................	6:00........................	6:00........................
7:00........................	7:00........................	7:00........................	7:00........................
8:00........................	8:00........................	8:00........................	8:00........................
9:00........................	9:00........................	9:00........................	9:00........................
10:00......................	10:00......................	10:00......................	10:00......................
11:00......................	11:00......................	11:00......................	11:00......................
12:00	12:00......................	12:00......................	12:00......................

MILESTONES REACHED

REFLECTION ON LAST WEEK

BIGGEST WINS OF LAST WEEK	THINGS TO BE GRATEFUL FOR
IDENTIFY TIME WASTERS	...AND HOW TO REDUCE AND ELIMINATE THEM
SELF-IMPROVEMENT IDEAS	GOALS FOR THE WEEK AHEAD

REWARD FOR HITTING GOALS

What worked?

What didn't work?

What needs improving?

What are my next actions?

"The tragedy in life doesn't lie in not reaching your goal. The tragedy lies in having no goal to reach."

Benjamin E Mays

SEPTEMBER

MONDAY	TUESDAY	WEDNESDAY	THURSDAY	FRIDAY	SATURDAY	SUNDAY
☐	☐	☐	☐	☐	☐	☐
MONDAY	TUESDAY	WEDNESDAY	THURSDAY	FRIDAY	SATURDAY	SUNDAY
☐	☐	☐	☐	☐	☐	☐
MONDAY	TUESDAY	WEDNESDAY	THURSDAY	FRIDAY	SATURDAY	SUNDAY
☐	☐	☐	☐	☐	☐	☐
MONDAY	TUESDAY	WEDNESDAY	THURSDAY	FRIDAY	SATURDAY	SUNDAY
☐	☐	☐	☐	☐	☐	☐

NOTES

MONTHLY GOALS

Month:

10 Goals	The 2 most important. Why?
1.	1º
2.	
3.	
4.	
5.	Deadline:
6.	2º
7.	
8.	
9.	
10.	Deadline:

WEEK: _____	MONDAY	TUESDAY	WEDNESDAY
Goal	Goal	Goal	Goal
SECUNDARY TASKS	Priorities	Priorities	Priorities

SECUNDARY TASKS	MONDAY Priorities	TUESDAY Priorities	WEDNESDAY Priorities
	1..	1..	1..
	2..	2..	2..
	.3..	3..	.
	.		3..
	6:00..	6:0	6:00..
	7:00..	7:0	7:00..
	8:00..	8:0	8:00..
	9:00..	9:0	9:00..
	10:00..	10:0	10:00..
ADITIONAL TASKS	11:00..	11:0	11:00..
	12:00..	12:0	12:00..
	1:00..	1:00..	1:00..
	2:00..	2:00..	2:00..
	.3:00..	3:00..	3:00..
	4:00..	4:00..	4:00..
	5:00..	5:00..	5:00..
	6:00..	6:00..	6:00..
	7:00..	7:00..	7:00..
	8:00..	8:00..	8:00..
	9:00..	9:00..	9:00..
	10:00..	10:00..	10:00..
	11:00..	11:00..	11:00..
	12:00..	12:00..	12:00..

HABIT TRACKER		M	T	W	T	F	S	S

THURSDAY	FRIDAY	SATURDAY	SUNDAY
Goal	Goal	Goal	Goal
Priorities	Priorities	Priorities	Priorities
1..	1..	1..	1..
2..	2..	2..	2..
.	.	.	.
3..	3..	3..	3..
6:00....................................	6:00....................................	6:00....................................	6:00....................................
7:00....................................	7:00....................................	7:00....................................	7:00....................................
8:00....................................	8:00....................................	8:00....................................	8:00....................................
9:00....................................	9:00....................................	9:00....................................	9:00....................................
10:00..................................	10:00..................................	10:00..................................	10:00..................................
11:00..................................	11:00..................................	11:00..................................	11:00..................................
12:00..................................	12:00..................................	12:00..................................	12:00..................................
1:00....................................	1:00....................................	1:00....................................	1:00....................................
2:00....................................	2:00....................................	2:00....................................	2:00....................................
3:00....................................	3:00....................................	3:00....................................	3:00....................................
4:00....................................	4:00....................................	4:00....................................	4:00....................................
5:00....................................	5:00....................................	5:00....................................	5:00....................................
6:00....................................	6:00....................................	6:00....................................	6:00....................................
7:00....................................	7:00....................................	7:00....................................	7:00....................................
8:00....................................	8:00....................................	8:00....................................	8:00....................................
9:00....................................	9:00....................................	9:00....................................	9:00....................................
10:00..................................	10:00..................................	10:00..................................	10:00..................................
11:00..................................	11:00..................................	11:00..................................	11:00..................................
12:00	12:00..................................	12:00..................................	12:00..................................

MILESTONES REACHED

REFLECTION ON LAST WEEK

BIGGEST WINS OF LAST WEEK	THINGS TO BE GRATEFUL FOR
IDENTIFY TIME WASTERS	...AND HOW TO REDUCE AND ELIMINATE THEM
SELF-IMPROVEMENT IDEAS	GOALS FOR THE WEEK AHEAD

REWARD FOR HITTING GOALS

What worked?

What didn't work?

What needs improving?

What are my next actions?

WEEK: _____	MONDAY	TUESDAY	WEDNESDAY
Goal	Goal	Goal	Goal
SECUNDARY TASKS	Priorities	Priorities	Priorities
	1.............................	1.............................	1.............................
	2.............................	2.............................	2.............................
	.3............................	3............................	.
	.		3............................
	6:00........................	6:0	6:00........................
	7:00........................	7:0	7:00........................
	8:00........................	8:0	8:00........................
	9:00........................	9:0	9:00........................
	10:00......................	10:0	10:00......................
ADITIONAL TASKS	11:00......................	11:0	11:00......................
	12:00......................	12:0	12:00......................
	1:00........................	1:00........................	1:00........................
	2:00........................	2:00........................	2:00........................
	.3:00.......................	3:00........................	3:00........................
	4:00........................	4:00........................	4:00........................
	5:00........................	5:00........................	5:00........................
	6:00........................	6:00........................	6:00........................
	7:00........................	7:00........................	7:00........................
	8:00........................	8:00........................	8:00........................
	9:00........................	9:00........................	9:00........................
	10:00......................	10:00......................	10:00......................
	11:00......................	11:00......................	11:00......................
	12:00......................	12:00......................	12:00......................

HABIT TRACKER	M	T	W	T	F	S	S

THURSDAY	FRIDAY	SATURDAY	SUNDAY
Goal	Goal	Goal	Goal
Priorities	Priorities	Priorities	Priorities
1..	1..	1..	1..
2..	2..	2..	2..
.	.	.	.
3..	3..	3..	3..
6:00....................................	6:00....................................	6:00....................................	6:00....................................
7:00....................................	7:00....................................	7:00....................................	7:00....................................
8:00....................................	8:00....................................	8:00....................................	8:00....................................
9:00....................................	9:00....................................	9:00....................................	9:00....................................
10:00..................................	10:00..................................	10:00..................................	10:00..................................
11:00..................................	11:00..................................	11:00..................................	11:00..................................
12:00..................................	12:00..................................	12:00..................................	12:00..................................
1:00....................................	1:00....................................	1:00....................................	1:00....................................
2:00....................................	2:00....................................	2:00....................................	2:00....................................
3:00....................................	3:00....................................	3:00....................................	3:00....................................
4:00....................................	4:00....................................	4:00....................................	4:00....................................
5:00....................................	5:00....................................	5:00....................................	5:00....................................
6:00....................................	6:00....................................	6:00....................................	6:00....................................
7:00....................................	7:00....................................	7:00....................................	7:00....................................
8:00....................................	8:00....................................	8:00....................................	8:00....................................
9:00....................................	9:00....................................	9:00....................................	9:00....................................
10:00..................................	10:00..................................	10:00..................................	10:00..................................
11:00..................................	11:00..................................	11:00..................................	11:00..................................
12:00	12:00..................................	12:00..................................	12:00..................................

MILESTONES REACHED

REFLECTION ON LAST WEEK

BIGGEST WINS OF LAST WEEK	THINGS TO BE GRATEFUL FOR
IDENTIFY TIME WASTERS	...AND HOW TO REDUCE AND ELIMINATE THEM
SELF-IMPROVEMENT IDEAS	GOALS FOR THE WEEK AHEAD

REWARD FOR HITTING GOALS

What worked?

What didn't work?

What needs improving?

What are my next actions?

WEEK: _____	MONDAY	TUESDAY	WEDNESDAY
Goal	Goal	Goal	Goal
SECUNDARY TASKS	Priorities	Priorities	Priorities

SECUNDARY TASKS	Priorities	Priorities	Priorities
	1...............................	1...............................	1...............................
	2...............................	2...............................	2...............................
	.3..............................	3...............................	.
	.		3...............................
	6:00........................	6:0	6:00........................
	7:00........................	7:0	7:00........................
	8:00........................	8:0	8:00........................
	9:00........................	9:0	9:00........................
	10:00......................	10:0	10:00......................
ADITIONAL TASKS	11:00......................	11:0	11:00......................
	12:00......................	12:0	12:00......................
	1:00........................	1:00........................	1:00........................
	2:00........................	2:00........................	2:00........................
	.3:00.......................	3:00........................	3:00........................
	4:00........................	4:00........................	4:00........................
	5:00........................	5:00........................	5:00........................
	6:00........................	6:00........................	6:00........................
	7:00........................	7:00........................	7:00........................
	8:00........................	8:00........................	8:00........................
	9:00........................	9:00........................	9:00........................
	10:00......................	10:00......................	10:00......................
	11:00......................	11:00......................	11:00......................
	12:00......................	12:00......................	12:00......................

HABIT TRACKER	M	T	W	T	F	S	S

THURSDAY	FRIDAY	SATURDAY	SUNDAY
Goal	Goal	Goal	Goal
Priorities	Priorities	Priorities	Priorities
1...............................	1...............................	1...............................	1...............................
2...............................	2...............................	2...............................	2...............................
.	.	.	.
3...............................	3...............................	3...............................	3...............................
6:00...............................	6:00...............................	6:00...............................	6:00...............................
7:00...............................	7:00...............................	7:00...............................	7:00...............................
8:00...............................	8:00...............................	8:00...............................	8:00...............................
9:00...............................	9:00...............................	9:00...............................	9:00...............................
10:00...............................	10:00...............................	10:00...............................	10:00...............................
11:00...............................	11:00...............................	11:00...............................	11:00...............................
12:00...............................	12:00...............................	12:00...............................	12:00...............................
1:00...............................	1:00...............................	1:00...............................	1:00...............................
2:00...............................	2:00...............................	2:00...............................	2:00...............................
3:00...............................	3:00...............................	3:00...............................	3:00...............................
4:00...............................	4:00...............................	4:00...............................	4:00...............................
5:00...............................	5:00...............................	5:00...............................	5:00...............................
6:00...............................	6:00...............................	6:00...............................	6:00...............................
7:00...............................	7:00...............................	7:00...............................	7:00...............................
8:00...............................	8:00...............................	8:00...............................	8:00...............................
9:00...............................	9:00...............................	9:00...............................	9:00...............................
10:00...............................	10:00...............................	10:00...............................	10:00...............................
11:00...............................	11:00...............................	11:00...............................	11:00...............................
12:00	12:00...............................	12:00...............................	12:00...............................

MILESTONES REACHED

REFLECTION ON LAST WEEK

BIGGEST WINS OF LAST WEEK	THINGS TO BE GRATEFUL FOR
IDENTIFY TIME WASTERS	...AND HOW TO REDUCE AND ELIMINATE THEM
SELF-IMPROVEMENT IDEAS	GOALS FOR THE WEEK AHEAD

REWARD FOR HITTING GOALS

What worked?

What didn't work?

What needs improving?

What are my next actions?

WEEK: _____	MONDAY	TUESDAY	WEDNESDAY
Goal	Goal	Goal	Goal
SECUNDARY TASKS	Priorities	Priorities	Priorities

SECUNDARY TASKS	Priorities	Priorities	Priorities
	1..	1..	1..
	2..	2..	2..
	3..	3..	.
	.		3..
	6:00..................................	6:0	6:00..................................
	7:00..................................	7:0	7:00..................................
	8:00..................................	8:0	8:00..................................
	9:00..................................	9:0	9:00..................................
	10:00................................	10:0	10:00................................
ADITIONAL TASKS	11:00................................	11:0	11:00................................
	12:00................................	12:0	12:00................................
	1:00..................................	1:00..................................	1:00..................................
	2:00..................................	2:00..................................	2:00..................................
	3:00..................................	3:00..................................	3:00..................................
	4:00..................................	4:00..................................	4:00..................................
	5:00..................................	5:00..................................	5:00..................................
	6:00..................................	6:00..................................	6:00..................................
	7:00..................................	7:00..................................	7:00..................................
	8:00..................................	8:00..................................	8:00..................................
	9:00..................................	9:00..................................	9:00..................................
	10:00................................	10:00................................	10:00................................
	11:00................................	11:00................................	11:00................................
	12:00................................	12:00................................	12:00................................

HABIT TRACKER	M	T	W	T	F	S	S

THURSDAY	FRIDAY	SATURDAY	SUNDAY
Goal	Goal	Goal	Goal
Priorities	Priorities	Priorities	Priorities
1..	1..	1..	1..
2..	2..	2..	2..
.	.	.	.
3..	3..	3..	3..
6:00......................................	6:00......................................	6:00......................................	6:00......................................
7:00......................................	7:00......................................	7:00......................................	7:00......................................
8:00......................................	8:00......................................	8:00......................................	8:00......................................
9:00......................................	9:00......................................	9:00......................................	9:00......................................
10:00....................................	10:00....................................	10:00....................................	10:00....................................
11:00....................................	11:00....................................	11:00....................................	11:00....................................
12:00....................................	12:00....................................	12:00....................................	12:00....................................
1:00......................................	1:00......................................	1:00......................................	1:00......................................
2:00......................................	2:00......................................	2:00......................................	2:00......................................
3:00......................................	3:00......................................	3:00......................................	3:00......................................
4:00......................................	4:00......................................	4:00......................................	4:00......................................
5:00......................................	5:00......................................	5:00......................................	5:00......................................
6:00......................................	6:00......................................	6:00......................................	6:00......................................
7:00......................................	7:00......................................	7:00......................................	7:00......................................
8:00......................................	8:00......................................	8:00......................................	8:00......................................
9:00......................................	9:00......................................	9:00......................................	9:00......................................
10:00....................................	10:00....................................	10:00....................................	10:00....................................
11:00....................................	11:00....................................	11:00....................................	11:00....................................
12:00	12:00....................................	12:00....................................	12:00....................................

MILESTONES REACHED

REFLECTION ON LAST WEEK

BIGGEST WINS OF LAST WEEK	THINGS TO BE GRATEFUL FOR
IDENTIFY TIME WASTERS	...AND HOW TO REDUCE AND ELIMINATE THEM
SELF-IMPROVEMENT IDEAS	GOALS FOR THE WEEK AHEAD

REWARD FOR HITTING GOALS

What worked?

What didn't work?

What needs improving?

What are my next actions?

"There are risks and costs to action. But they are far less than the long-range risks of comfortable inaction."

John F. Kennedy

OCTOBER

MONDAY	TUESDAY	WEDNESDAY	THURSDAY	FRIDAY	SATURDAY	SUNDAY
☐	☐	☐	☐	☐	☐	☐

MONDAY	TUESDAY	WEDNESDAY	THURSDAY	FRIDAY	SATURDAY	SUNDAY
☐	☐	☐	☐	☐	☐	☐

MONDAY	TUESDAY	WEDNESDAY	THURSDAY	FRIDAY	SATURDAY	SUNDAY
☐	☐	☐	☐	☐	☐	☐

MONDAY	TUESDAY	WEDNESDAY	THURSDAY	FRIDAY	SATURDAY	SUNDAY
☐	☐	☐	☐	☐	☐	☐

NOTES

MONTHLY GOALS

Month:

10 Goals	The 2 most important. Why?
1.	**1º**
2.	
3.	
4.	
5.	
	Deadline:
6.	**2º**
7.	
8.	
9.	
10.	Deadline:

WEEK: _____	MONDAY	TUESDAY	WEDNESDAY
Goal	Goal	Goal	Goal
SECUNDARY TASKS	Priorities	Priorities	Priorities
	1..	1..	1..
	2..	2..	2..
	.3...	3..	.
	.		3..
	6:00..	6:0	6:00..
	7:00..	7:0	7:00..
	8:00..	8:0	8:00..
	9:00..	9:0	9:00..
	10:00......................................	10:0	10:00......................................
ADITIONAL TASKS	11:00......................................	11:0	11:00......................................
	12:00......................................	12:0	12:00......................................
	1:00..	1:00..	1:00..
	2:00..	2:00..	2:00..
	.3:00.......................................	3:00..	3:00..
	4:00..	4:00..	4:00..
	5:00..	5:00..	5:00..
	6:00..	6:00..	6:00..
	7:00..	7:00..	7:00..
	8:00..	8:00..	8:00..
	9:00..	9:00..	9:00..
	10:00......................................	10:00......................................	10:00......................................
	11:00......................................	11:00......................................	11:00......................................
	12:00......................................	12:00......................................	12:00......................................

HABIT TRACKER	M	T	W	T	F	S	S

THURSDAY	FRIDAY	SATURDAY	SUNDAY
Goal	Goal	Goal	Goal
Priorities	Priorities	Priorities	Priorities
1..	1..	1..	1..
2..	2..	2..	2..
.	.	.	.
3..	3..	3..	3..
6:00..	6:00..	6:00..	6:00..
7:00..	7:00..	7:00..	7:00..
8:00..	8:00..	8:00..	8:00..
9:00..	9:00..	9:00..	9:00..
10:00..	10:00..	10:00..	10:00..
11:00..	11:00..	11:00..	11:00..
12:00..	12:00..	12:00..	12:00..
1:00..	1:00..	1:00..	1:00..
2:00..	2:00..	2:00..	2:00..
3:00..	3:00..	3:00..	3:00..
4:00..	4:00..	4:00..	4:00..
5:00..	5:00..	5:00..	5:00..
6:00..	6:00..	6:00..	6:00..
7:00..	7:00..	7:00..	7:00..
8:00..	8:00..	8:00..	8:00..
9:00..	9:00..	9:00..	9:00..
10:00..	10:00..	10:00..	10:00..
11:00..	11:00..	11:00..	11:00..
12:00..	12:00..	12:00..	12:00..

MILESTONES REACHED

REFLECTION ON LAST WEEK

BIGGEST WINS OF LAST WEEK	THINGS TO BE GRATEFUL FOR
IDENTIFY TIME WASTERS	...AND HOW TO REDUCE AND ELIMINATE THEM
SELF-IMPROVEMENT IDEAS	GOALS FOR THE WEEK AHEAD

REWARD FOR HITTING GOALS

What worked?

What didn't work?

What needs improving?

What are my next actions?

WEEK: _____	MONDAY	TUESDAY	WEDNESDAY
Goal	Goal	Goal	Goal
SECUNDARY TASKS	Priorities	Priorities	Priorities

SECUNDARY TASKS	Priorities	Priorities	Priorities
	1..........................	1..........................	1..........................
	2..........................	2..........................	2..........................
	.3..........................	3..........................	.
	.		3..........................
	6:00..........................	6:0	6:00..........................
	7:00..........................	7:0	7:00..........................
	8:00..........................	8:0	8:00..........................
	9:00..........................	9:0	9:00..........................
	10:00..........................	10:0	10:00..........................
ADITIONAL TASKS	11:00..........................	11:0	11:00..........................
	12:00..........................	12:0	12:00..........................
	1:00..........................	1:00..........................	1:00..........................
	2:00..........................	2:00..........................	2:00..........................
	.3:00..........................	3:00..........................	3:00..........................
	4:00..........................	4:00..........................	4:00..........................
	5:00..........................	5:00..........................	5:00..........................
	6:00..........................	6:00..........................	6:00..........................
	7:00..........................	7:00..........................	7:00..........................
	8:00..........................	8:00..........................	8:00..........................
	9:00..........................	9:00..........................	9:00..........................
	10:00..........................	10:00..........................	10:00..........................
	11:00..........................	11:00..........................	11:00..........................
	12:00..........................	12:00..........................	12:00..........................

HABIT TRACKER	M	T	W	T	F	S	S

THURSDAY	FRIDAY	SATURDAY	SUNDAY
Goal	Goal	Goal	Goal
Priorities	Priorities	Priorities	Priorities
1........................	1........................	1........................	1........................
2........................	2........................	2........................	2........................
.	.	.	.
3........................	3........................	3........................	3........................
6:00....................	6:00....................	6:00....................	6:00....................
7:00....................	7:00....................	7:00....................	7:00....................
8:00....................	8:00....................	8:00....................	8:00....................
9:00....................	9:00....................	9:00....................	9:00....................
10:00..................	10:00..................	10:00..................	10:00..................
11:00..................	11:00..................	11:00..................	11:00..................
12:00..................	12:00..................	12:00..................	12:00..................
1:00....................	1:00....................	1:00....................	1:00....................
2:00....................	2:00....................	2:00....................	2:00....................
3:00....................	3:00....................	3:00....................	3:00....................
4:00....................	4:00....................	4:00....................	4:00....................
5:00....................	5:00....................	5:00....................	5:00....................
6:00....................	6:00....................	6:00....................	6:00....................
7:00....................	7:00....................	7:00....................	7:00....................
8:00....................	8:00....................	8:00....................	8:00....................
9:00....................	9:00....................	9:00....................	9:00....................
10:00..................	10:00..................	10:00..................	10:00..................
11:00..................	11:00..................	11:00..................	11:00..................
12:00	12:00..................	12:00..................	12:00..................

MILESTONES REACHED

REFLECTION ON LAST WEEK

BIGGEST WINS OF LAST WEEK	THINGS TO BE GRATEFUL FOR
IDENTIFY TIME WASTERS	...AND HOW TO REDUCE AND ELIMINATE THEM
SELF-IMPROVEMENT IDEAS	GOALS FOR THE WEEK AHEAD

REWARD FOR HITTING GOALS

What worked?

What didn't work?

What needs improving?

What are my next actions?

WEEK: _____	MONDAY	TUESDAY	WEDNESDAY
Goal	Goal	Goal	Goal
SECUNDARY TASKS	Priorities	Priorities	Priorities
	1..	1..	1..
	2..	2..	2..
	.3..	3..	.
	.		3..
	6:00..	6:0	6:00..
	7:00..	7:0	7:00..
	8:00..	8:0	8:00..
	9:00..	9:0	9:00..
	10:00..	10:0	10:00..
ADITIONAL TASKS	11:00..	11:0	11:00..
	12:00..	12:0	12:00..
	1:00..	1:00..	1:00..
	2:00..	2:00..	2:00..
	.3:00..	3:00..	3:00..
	4:00..	4:00..	4:00..
	5:00..	5:00..	5:00..
	6:00..	6:00..	6:00..
	7:00..	7:00..	7:00..
	8:00..	8:00..	8:00..
	9:00..	9:00..	9:00..
	10:00..	10:00..	10:00..
	11:00..	11:00..	11:00..
	12:00..	12:00..	12:00..

HABIT TRACKER		M	T	W	T	F	S	S

THURSDAY	FRIDAY	SATURDAY	SUNDAY
Goal	Goal	Goal	Goal
Priorities	Priorities	Priorities	Priorities
1.........................	1.........................	1.........................	1.........................
2.........................	2.........................	2.........................	2.........................
.	.	.	.
3.........................	3.........................	3.........................	3.........................
6:00.........................	6:00.........................	6:00.........................	6:00.........................
7:00.........................	7:00.........................	7:00.........................	7:00.........................
8:00.........................	8:00.........................	8:00.........................	8:00.........................
9:00.........................	9:00.........................	9:00.........................	9:00.........................
10:00.........................	10:00.........................	10:00.........................	10:00.........................
11:00.........................	11:00.........................	11:00.........................	11:00.........................
12:00.........................	12:00.........................	12:00.........................	12:00.........................
1:00.........................	1:00.........................	1:00.........................	1:00.........................
2:00.........................	2:00.........................	2:00.........................	2:00.........................
3:00.........................	3:00.........................	3:00.........................	3:00.........................
4:00.........................	4:00.........................	4:00.........................	4:00.........................
5:00.........................	5:00.........................	5:00.........................	5:00.........................
6:00.........................	6:00.........................	6:00.........................	6:00.........................
7:00.........................	7:00.........................	7:00.........................	7:00.........................
8:00.........................	8:00.........................	8:00.........................	8:00.........................
9:00.........................	9:00.........................	9:00.........................	9:00.........................
10:00.........................	10:00.........................	10:00.........................	10:00.........................
11:00.........................	11:00.........................	11:00.........................	11:00.........................
12:00	12:00.........................	12:00.........................	12:00.........................

MILESTONES REACHED

_____

_____

_____

_____

_____

REFLECTION ON LAST WEEK

BIGGEST WINS OF LAST WEEK	THINGS TO BE GRATEFUL FOR
IDENTIFY TIME WASTERS	...AND HOW TO REDUCE AND ELIMINATE THEM
SELF-IMPROVEMENT IDEAS	GOALS FOR THE WEEK AHEAD

REWARD FOR HITTING GOALS

What worked?

What didn't work?

What needs improving?

What are my next actions?

WEEK: _____	MONDAY	TUESDAY	WEDNESDAY
Goal	Goal	Goal	Goal
SECUNDARY TASKS	Priorities	Priorities	Priorities
	1....................................	1....................................	1....................................
	2....................................	2....................................	2....................................
	3....................................	3....................................	.
	.		3....................................
	6:00................................	6:0	6:00................................
	7:00................................	7:0	7:00................................
	8:00................................	8:0	8:00................................
	9:00................................	9:0	9:00................................
	10:00..............................	10:0	10:00..............................
ADITIONAL TASKS	11:00..............................	11:0	11:00..............................
	12:00..............................	12:0	12:00..............................
	1:00................................	1:00................................	1:00................................
	2:00................................	2:00................................	2:00................................
	3:00................................	3:00................................	3:00................................
	4:00................................	4:00................................	4:00................................
	5:00................................	5:00................................	5:00................................
	6:00................................	6:00................................	6:00................................
	7:00................................	7:00................................	7:00................................
	8:00................................	8:00................................	8:00................................
	9:00................................	9:00................................	9:00................................
	10:00..............................	10:00..............................	10:00..............................
	11:00..............................	11:00..............................	11:00..............................
	12:00..............................	12:00..............................	12:00..............................

HABIT TRACKER		M	T	W	T	F	S	S

THURSDAY	FRIDAY	SATURDAY	SUNDAY
Goal	Goal	Goal	Goal
Priorities	Priorities	Priorities	Priorities
1...	1...	1...	1...
2...	2...	2...	2...
.	.	.	.
3...	3...	3...	3...
6:00...	6:00...	6:00...	6:00...
7:00...	7:00...	7:00...	7:00...
8:00...	8:00...	8:00...	8:00...
9:00...	9:00...	9:00...	9:00...
10:00...	10:00...	10:00...	10:00...
11:00...	11:00...	11:00...	11:00...
12:00...	12:00...	12:00...	12:00...
1:00...	1:00...	1:00...	1:00...
2:00...	2:00...	2:00...	2:00...
3:00...	3:00...	3:00...	3:00...
4:00...	4:00...	4:00...	4:00...
5:00...	5:00...	5:00...	5:00...
6:00...	6:00...	6:00...	6:00...
7:00...	7:00...	7:00...	7:00...
8:00...	8:00...	8:00...	8:00...
9:00...	9:00...	9:00...	9:00...
10:00...	10:00...	10:00...	10:00...
11:00...	11:00...	11:00...	11:00...
12:00...	12:00...	12:00...	12:00...

MILESTONES REACHED

REFLECTION ON LAST WEEK

BIGGEST WINS OF LAST WEEK	THINGS TO BE GRATEFUL FOR
IDENTIFY TIME WASTERS	...AND HOW TO REDUCE AND ELIMINATE THEM
SELF-IMPROVEMENT IDEAS	GOALS FOR THE WEEK AHEAD

REWARD FOR HITTING GOALS

What worked?

What didn't work?

What needs improving?

What are my next actions?

NOVEMBER

MONDAY	TUESDAY	WEDNESDAY	THURSDAY	FRIDAY	SATURDAY	SUNDAY
☐	☐	☐	☐	☐	☐	☐
MONDAY	TUESDAY	WEDNESDAY	THURSDAY	FRIDAY	SATURDAY	SUNDAY
☐	☐	☐	☐	☐	☐	☐
MONDAY	TUESDAY	WEDNESDAY	THURSDAY	FRIDAY	SATURDAY	SUNDAY
☐	☐	☐	☐	☐	☐	☐
MONDAY	TUESDAY	WEDNESDAY	THURSDAY	FRIDAY	SATURDAY	SUNDAY
☐	☐	☐	☐	☐	☐	☐

NOTES

MONTHLY GOALS

Month:

10 Goals	The 2 most important. Why?
1.	**1º**
2.	
3.	
4.	
5.	
	Deadline:
6.	**2º**
7.	
8.	
9.	
10.	Deadline:

WEEK: _____	MONDAY	TUESDAY	WEDNESDAY
Goal	Goal	Goal	Goal
SECUNDARY TASKS	Priorities	Priorities	Priorities
	1............................	1............................	1............................
	2............................	2............................	2............................
	3............................	3............................	.
	.		3............................
	6:00......................	6:0	6:00......................
	7:00......................	7:0	7:00......................
	8:00......................	8:0	8:00......................
	9:00......................	9:0	9:00......................
	10:00....................	10:0	10:00....................
ADITIONAL TASKS	11:00....................	11:0	11:00....................
	12:00....................	12:0	12:00....................
	1:00......................	1:00......................	1:00......................
	2:00......................	2:00......................	2:00......................
	3:00......................	3:00......................	3:00......................
	4:00......................	4:00......................	4:00......................
	5:00......................	5:00......................	5:00......................
	6:00......................	6:00......................	6:00......................
	7:00......................	7:00......................	7:00......................
	8:00......................	8:00......................	8:00......................
	9:00......................	9:00......................	9:00......................
	10:00....................	10:00....................	10:00....................
	11:00....................	11:00....................	11:00....................
	12:00....................	12:00....................	12:00....................

HABIT TRACKER			M	T	W	T	F	S	S

THURSDAY	FRIDAY	SATURDAY	SUNDAY
Goal	Goal	Goal	Goal
Priorities	Priorities	Priorities	Priorities
1..	1..	1..	1..
2..	2..	2..	2..
.	.	.	.
3..	3..	3..	3..
6:00....................................	6:00....................................	6:00....................................	6:00....................................
7:00....................................	7:00....................................	7:00....................................	7:00....................................
8:00....................................	8:00....................................	8:00....................................	8:00....................................
9:00....................................	9:00....................................	9:00....................................	9:00....................................
10:00..................................	10:00..................................	10:00..................................	10:00..................................
11:00..................................	11:00..................................	11:00..................................	11:00..................................
12:00..................................	12:00..................................	12:00..................................	12:00..................................
1:00....................................	1:00....................................	1:00....................................	1:00....................................
2:00....................................	2:00....................................	2:00....................................	2:00....................................
3:00....................................	3:00....................................	3:00....................................	3:00....................................
4:00....................................	4:00....................................	4:00....................................	4:00....................................
5:00....................................	5:00....................................	5:00....................................	5:00....................................
6:00....................................	6:00....................................	6:00....................................	6:00....................................
7:00....................................	7:00....................................	7:00....................................	7:00....................................
8:00....................................	8:00....................................	8:00....................................	8:00....................................
9:00....................................	9:00....................................	9:00....................................	9:00....................................
10:00..................................	10:00..................................	10:00..................................	10:00..................................
11:00..................................	11:00..................................	11:00..................................	11:00..................................
12:00	12:00..................................	12:00..................................	12:00..................................

MILESTONES REACHED

REFLECTION ON LAST WEEK

BIGGEST WINS OF LAST WEEK	THINGS TO BE GRATEFUL FOR
IDENTIFY TIME WASTERS	...AND HOW TO REDUCE AND ELIMINATE THEM
SELF-IMPROVEMENT IDEAS	GOALS FOR THE WEEK AHEAD

REWARD FOR HITTING GOALS

What worked?

What didn't work?

What needs improving?

What are my next actions?

WEEK: _____	MONDAY	TUESDAY	WEDNESDAY
Goal	Goal	Goal	Goal
SECUNDARY TASKS	Priorities	Priorities	Priorities
	1.......................	1.......................	1.......................
	2.......................	2.......................	2.......................
	.3.......................	3.......................	.
	.		3.......................
	6:00.......................	6:0	6:00.......................
	7:00.......................	7:0	7:00.......................
	8:00.......................	8:0	8:00.......................
	9:00.......................	9:0	9:00.......................
	10:00.......................	10:0	10:00.......................
ADITIONAL TASKS	11:00.......................	11:0	11:00.......................
	12:00.......................	12:0	12:00.......................
	1:00.......................	1:00.......................	1:00.......................
	2:00.......................	2:00.......................	2:00.......................
	.3:00.......................	3:00.......................	3:00.......................
	4:00.......................	4:00.......................	4:00.......................
	5:00.......................	5:00.......................	5:00.......................
	6:00.......................	6:00.......................	6:00.......................
	7:00.......................	7:00.......................	7:00.......................
	8:00.......................	8:00.......................	8:00.......................
	9:00.......................	9:00.......................	9:00.......................
	10:00.......................	10:00.......................	10:00.......................
	11:00.......................	11:00.......................	11:00.......................
	12:00.......................	12:00.......................	12:00.......................

HABIT TRACKER		M	T	W	T	F	S	S

THURSDAY	FRIDAY	SATURDAY	SUNDAY
Goal	Goal	Goal	Goal
Priorities	Priorities	Priorities	Priorities
1...............................	1...............................	1...............................	1...............................
2...............................	2...............................	2...............................	2...............................
.	.	.	.
3...............................	3...............................	3...............................	3...............................
6:00............................	6:00............................	6:00............................	6:00............................
7:00............................	7:00............................	7:00............................	7:00............................
8:00............................	8:00............................	8:00............................	8:00............................
9:00............................	9:00............................	9:00............................	9:00............................
10:00..........................	10:00..........................	10:00..........................	10:00..........................
11:00..........................	11:00..........................	11:00..........................	11:00..........................
12:00..........................	12:00..........................	12:00..........................	12:00..........................
1:00............................	1:00............................	1:00............................	1:00............................
2:00............................	2:00............................	2:00............................	2:00............................
3:00............................	3:00............................	3:00............................	3:00............................
4:00............................	4:00............................	4:00............................	4:00............................
5:00............................	5:00............................	5:00............................	5:00............................
6:00............................	6:00............................	6:00............................	6:00............................
7:00............................	7:00............................	7:00............................	7:00............................
8:00............................	8:00............................	8:00............................	8:00............................
9:00............................	9:00............................	9:00............................	9:00............................
10:00..........................	10:00..........................	10:00..........................	10:00..........................
11:00..........................	11:00..........................	11:00..........................	11:00..........................
12:00	12:00..........................	12:00..........................	12:00..........................
MILESTONES REACHED			

REFLECTION ON LAST WEEK

BIGGEST WINS OF LAST WEEK	THINGS TO BE GRATEFUL FOR
IDENTIFY TIME WASTERS	...AND HOW TO REDUCE AND ELIMINATE THEM
SELF-IMPROVEMENT IDEAS	GOALS FOR THE WEEK AHEAD

REWARD FOR HITTING GOALS

What worked?

What didn't work?

What needs improving?

What are my next actions?

WEEK: _____	MONDAY	TUESDAY	WEDNESDAY
Goal	Goal	Goal	Goal
SECUNDARY TASKS	Priorities	Priorities	Priorities
	1...	1...	1...
	2...	2...	2...
	.3..	3...	.
	.		3...
	6:00...	6:0	6:00...
	7:00...	7:0	7:00...
	8:00...	8:0	8:00...
	9:00...	9:0	9:00...
	10:00.......................................	10:0	10:00.......................................
ADITIONAL TASKS	11:00.......................................	11:0	11:00.......................................
	12:00.......................................	12:0	12:00.......................................
	1:00...	1:00...	1:00...
	2:00...	2:00...	2:00...
	.3:00..	3:00...	3:00...
	4:00...	4:00...	4:00...
	5:00...	5:00...	5:00...
	6:00...	6:00...	6:00...
	7:00...	7:00...	7:00...
	8:00...	8:00...	8:00...
	9:00...	9:00...	9:00...
	10:00.......................................	10:00.......................................	10:00.......................................
	11:00.......................................	11:00.......................................	11:00.......................................
	12:00.......................................	12:00.......................................	12:00.......................................

HABIT TRACKER			M	T	W	T	F	S	S

THURSDAY	FRIDAY	SATURDAY	SUNDAY
Goal	Goal	Goal	Goal
Priorities	Priorities	Priorities	Priorities
1...............................	1...............................	1...............................	1...............................
2...............................	2...............................	2...............................	2...............................
.	.	.	.
3...............................	3...............................	3...............................	3...............................
6:00..........................	6:00..........................	6:00..........................	6:00..........................
7:00..........................	7:00..........................	7:00..........................	7:00..........................
8:00..........................	8:00..........................	8:00..........................	8:00..........................
9:00..........................	9:00..........................	9:00..........................	9:00..........................
10:00........................	10:00........................	10:00........................	10:00........................
11:00........................	11:00........................	11:00........................	11:00........................
12:00........................	12:00........................	12:00........................	12:00........................
1:00..........................	1:00..........................	1:00..........................	1:00..........................
2:00..........................	2:00..........................	2:00..........................	2:00..........................
3:00..........................	3:00..........................	3:00..........................	3:00..........................
4:00..........................	4:00..........................	4:00..........................	4:00..........................
5:00..........................	5:00..........................	5:00..........................	5:00..........................
6:00..........................	6:00..........................	6:00..........................	6:00..........................
7:00..........................	7:00..........................	7:00..........................	7:00..........................
8:00..........................	8:00..........................	8:00..........................	8:00..........................
9:00..........................	9:00..........................	9:00..........................	9:00..........................
10:00........................	10:00........................	10:00........................	10:00........................
11:00........................	11:00........................	11:00........................	11:00........................
12:00	12:00........................	12:00........................	12:00........................

MILESTONES REACHED

REFLECTION ON LAST WEEK

BIGGEST WINS OF LAST WEEK	THINGS TO BE GRATEFUL FOR
IDENTIFY TIME WASTERS	...AND HOW TO REDUCE AND ELIMINATE THEM
SELF-IMPROVEMENT IDEAS	GOALS FOR THE WEEK AHEAD

REWARD FOR HITTING GOALS

What worked?

What didn't work?

What needs improving?

What are my next actions?

WEEK: _____	MONDAY	TUESDAY	WEDNESDAY
Goal	Goal	Goal	Goal

SECUNDARY TASKS	Priorities	Priorities	Priorities
	1..	1..	1..
	2..	2..	2..
	3..	3..	.
	.		3..

	MONDAY	TUESDAY	WEDNESDAY
	6:00........................	6:0	6:00........................
	7:00........................	7:0	7:00........................
	8:00........................	8:0	8:00........................
	9:00........................	9:0	9:00........................
	10:00........................	10:0	10:00........................
ADITIONAL TASKS	11:00........................	11:0	11:00........................
	12:00........................	12:0	12:00........................
	1:00........................	1:00........................	1:00........................
	2:00........................	2:00........................	2:00........................
	3:00........................	3:00........................	3:00........................
	4:00........................	4:00........................	4:00........................
	5:00........................	5:00........................	5:00........................
	6:00........................	6:00........................	6:00........................
	7:00........................	7:00........................	7:00........................
	8:00........................	8:00........................	8:00........................
	9:00........................	9:00........................	9:00........................
	10:00........................	10:00........................	10:00........................
	11:00........................	11:00........................	11:00........................
	12:00........................	12:00........................	12:00........................

HABIT TRACKER			M	T	W	T	F	S	S

THURSDAY	FRIDAY	SATURDAY	SUNDAY
Goal	Goal	Goal	Goal
Priorities	Priorities	Priorities	Priorities
1..	1..	1..	1..
2..	2..	2..	2..
.	.	.	.
3..	3..	3..	3..
6:00..	6:00..	6:00..	6:00..
7:00..	7:00..	7:00..	7:00..
8:00..	8:00..	8:00..	8:00..
9:00..	9:00..	9:00..	9:00..
10:00......................................	10:00......................................	10:00......................................	10:00......................................
11:00......................................	11:00......................................	11:00......................................	11:00......................................
12:00......................................	12:00......................................	12:00......................................	12:00......................................
1:00..	1:00..	1:00..	1:00..
2:00..	2:00..	2:00..	2:00..
3:00..	3:00..	3:00..	3:00..
4:00..	4:00..	4:00..	4:00..
5:00..	5:00..	5:00..	5:00..
6:00..	6:00..	6:00..	6:00..
7:00..	7:00..	7:00..	7:00..
8:00..	8:00..	8:00..	8:00..
9:00..	9:00..	9:00..	9:00..
10:00......................................	10:00......................................	10:00......................................	10:00......................................
11:00......................................	11:00......................................	11:00......................................	11:00......................................
12:00	12:00......................................	12:00......................................	12:00......................................

MILESTONES REACHED

REFLECTION ON LAST WEEK

BIGGEST WINS OF LAST WEEK	THINGS TO BE GRATEFUL FOR
IDENTIFY TIME WASTERS	...AND HOW TO REDUCE AND ELIMINATE THEM
SELF-IMPROVEMENT IDEAS	GOALS FOR THE WEEK AHEAD

REWARD FOR HITTING GOALS

What worked?

What didn't work?

What needs improving?

What are my next actions?

"Efficiency is doing things right. Effectiveness is doing the right things."

Peter Drucker

DECEMBER

MONTH: _____

MONDAY	TUESDAY	WEDNESDAY	THURSDAY	FRIDAY	SATURDAY	SUNDAY
☐	☐	☐	☐	☐	☐	☐

MONDAY	TUESDAY	WEDNESDAY	THURSDAY	FRIDAY	SATURDAY	SUNDAY
☐	☐	☐	☐	☐	☐	☐

MONDAY	TUESDAY	WEDNESDAY	THURSDAY	FRIDAY	SATURDAY	SUNDAY
☐	☐	☐	☐	☐	☐	☐

MONDAY	TUESDAY	WEDNESDAY	THURSDAY	FRIDAY	SATURDAY	SUNDAY
☐	☐	☐	☐	☐	☐	☐

NOTES

MONTHLY GOALS

Month:

10 Goals	The 2 most important. Why?
1.	1º
2.	
3.	
4.	
5.	Deadline:
6.	2º
7.	
8.	
9.	
10.	Deadline:

WEEK:_____	MONDAY	TUESDAY	WEDNESDAY
Goal	Goal	Goal	Goal
SECUNDARY TASKS	Priorities	Priorities	Priorities
	1...	1...	1...
	2...	2...	2...
	3...	3...	.
	.		3...
	6:00..	6:0	6:00..
	7:00..	7:0	7:00..
	8:00..	8:0	8:00..
	9:00..	9:0	9:00..
	10:00..	10:0	10:00..
ADITIONAL TASKS	11:00..	11:0	11:00..
	12:00..	12:0	12:00..
	1:00..	1:00..	1:00..
	2:00..	2:00..	2:00..
	.3:00...	3:00..	3:00..
	4:00..	4:00..	4:00..
	5:00..	5:00..	5:00..
	6:00..	6:00..	6:00..
	7:00..	7:00..	7:00..
	8:00..	8:00..	8:00..
	9:00..	9:00..	9:00..
	10:00..	10:00..	10:00..
	11:00..	11:00..	11:00..
	12:00..	12:00..	12:00..

HABIT TRACKER	M	T	W	T	F	S	S

THURSDAY	FRIDAY	SATURDAY	SUNDAY
Goal	Goal	Goal	Goal
Priorities	Priorities	Priorities	Priorities
1.........................	1.........................	1.........................	1.........................
2.........................	2.........................	2.........................	2.........................
.	.	.	.
3.........................	3.........................	3.........................	3.........................
6:00.....................	6:00.....................	6:00.....................	6:00.....................
7:00.....................	7:00.....................	7:00.....................	7:00.....................
8:00.....................	8:00.....................	8:00.....................	8:00.....................
9:00.....................	9:00.....................	9:00.....................	9:00.....................
10:00...................	10:00...................	10:00...................	10:00...................
11:00...................	11:00...................	11:00...................	11:00...................
12:00...................	12:00...................	12:00...................	12:00...................
1:00.....................	1:00.....................	1:00.....................	1:00.....................
2:00.....................	2:00.....................	2:00.....................	2:00.....................
3:00.....................	3:00.....................	3:00.....................	3:00.....................
4:00.....................	4:00.....................	4:00.....................	4:00.....................
5:00.....................	5:00.....................	5:00.....................	5:00.....................
6:00.....................	6:00.....................	6:00.....................	6:00.....................
7:00.....................	7:00.....................	7:00.....................	7:00.....................
8:00.....................	8:00.....................	8:00.....................	8:00.....................
9:00.....................	9:00.....................	9:00.....................	9:00.....................
10:00...................	10:00...................	10:00...................	10:00...................
11:00...................	11:00...................	11:00...................	11:00...................
12:00	12:00...................	12:00...................	12:00...................

MILESTONES REACHED

REFLECTION ON LAST WEEK

BIGGEST WINS OF LAST WEEK	THINGS TO BE GRATEFUL FOR
IDENTIFY TIME WASTERS	...AND HOW TO REDUCE AND ELIMINATE THEM
SELF-IMPROVEMENT IDEAS	GOALS FOR THE WEEK AHEAD

REWARD FOR HITTING GOALS

What worked?

What didn't work?

What needs improving?

What are my next actions?

WEEK: _____	MONDAY	TUESDAY	WEDNESDAY
Goal	Goal	Goal	Goal
SECUNDARY TASKS	Priorities	Priorities	Priorities
	1............................	1............................	1............................
	2............................	2............................	2............................
	.3...........................	3............................	.
	.		3............................
	6:00........................	6:0	6:00........................
	7:00........................	7:0	7:00........................
	8:00........................	8:0	8:00........................
	9:00........................	9:0	9:00........................
	10:00......................	10:0	10:00......................
ADITIONAL TASKS	11:00......................	11:0	11:00......................
	12:00......................	12:0	12:00......................
	1:00........................	1:00........................	1:00........................
	2:00........................	2:00........................	2:00........................
	.3:00.......................	3:00........................	3:00........................
	4:00........................	4:00........................	4:00........................
	5:00........................	5:00........................	5:00........................
	6:00........................	6:00........................	6:00........................
	7:00........................	7:00........................	7:00........................
	8:00........................	8:00........................	8:00........................
	9:00........................	9:00........................	9:00........................
	10:00......................	10:00......................	10:00......................
	11:00......................	11:00......................	11:00......................
	12:00......................	12:00......................	12:00......................

HABIT TRACKER			M	T	W	T	F	S	S

THURSDAY	FRIDAY	SATURDAY	SUNDAY
Goal	Goal	Goal	Goal
Priorities	Priorities	Priorities	Priorities
1....................................	1....................................	1....................................	1....................................
2....................................	2....................................	2....................................	2....................................
.	.	.	.
3....................................	3....................................	3....................................	3....................................
6:00.................................	6:00.................................	6:00.................................	6:00.................................
7:00.................................	7:00.................................	7:00.................................	7:00.................................
8:00.................................	8:00.................................	8:00.................................	8:00.................................
9:00.................................	9:00.................................	9:00.................................	9:00.................................
10:00...............................	10:00...............................	10:00...............................	10:00...............................
11:00...............................	11:00...............................	11:00...............................	11:00...............................
12:00...............................	12:00...............................	12:00...............................	12:00...............................
1:00.................................	1:00.................................	1:00.................................	1:00.................................
2:00.................................	2:00.................................	2:00.................................	2:00.................................
3:00.................................	3:00.................................	3:00.................................	3:00.................................
4:00.................................	4:00.................................	4:00.................................	4:00.................................
5:00.................................	5:00.................................	5:00.................................	5:00.................................
6:00.................................	6:00.................................	6:00.................................	6:00.................................
7:00.................................	7:00.................................	7:00.................................	7:00.................................
8:00.................................	8:00.................................	8:00.................................	8:00.................................
9:00.................................	9:00.................................	9:00.................................	9:00.................................
10:00...............................	10:00...............................	10:00...............................	10:00...............................
11:00...............................	11:00...............................	11:00...............................	11:00...............................
12:00	12:00...............................	12:00...............................	12:00...............................

MILESTONES REACHED

REFLECTION ON LAST WEEK

BIGGEST WINS OF LAST WEEK	THINGS TO BE GRATEFUL FOR
IDENTIFY TIME WASTERS	...AND HOW TO REDUCE AND ELIMINATE THEM
SELF-IMPROVEMENT IDEAS	GOALS FOR THE WEEK AHEAD

REWARD FOR HITTING GOALS

What worked?

What didn't work?

What needs improving?

What are my next actions?

WEEK: _____	MONDAY	TUESDAY	WEDNESDAY
Goal	Goal	Goal	Goal
SECUNDARY TASKS	Priorities	Priorities	Priorities
	1...............................	1...............................	1...............................
	2...............................	2...............................	2...............................
	3...............................	3...............................	.
	.		3...............................
	6:00............................	6:0	6:00............................
	7:00............................	7:0	7:00............................
	8:00............................	8:0	8:00............................
	9:00............................	9:0	9:00............................
	10:00..........................	10:0	10:00..........................
ADITIONAL TASKS	11:00..........................	11:0	11:00..........................
	12:00..........................	12:0	12:00..........................
	1:00............................	1:00............................	1:00............................
	2:00............................	2:00............................	2:00............................
	3:00............................	3:00............................	3:00............................
	4:00............................	4:00............................	4:00............................
	5:00............................	5:00............................	5:00............................
	6:00............................	6:00............................	6:00............................
	7:00............................	7:00............................	7:00............................
	8:00............................	8:00............................	8:00............................
	9:00............................	9:00............................	9:00............................
	10:00..........................	10:00..........................	10:00..........................
	11:00..........................	11:00..........................	11:00..........................
	12:00..........................	12:00..........................	12:00..........................

HABIT TRACKER		M	T	W	T	F	S	S

THURSDAY	FRIDAY	SATURDAY	SUNDAY
Goal	Goal	Goal	Goal
Priorities	Priorities	Priorities	Priorities
1...	1...	1...	1...
2...	2...	2...	2...
.	.	.	.
3...	3...	3...	3...
6:00..................................	6:00..................................	6:00..................................	6:00..................................
7:00..................................	7:00..................................	7:00..................................	7:00..................................
8:00..................................	8:00..................................	8:00..................................	8:00..................................
9:00..................................	9:00..................................	9:00..................................	9:00..................................
10:00................................	10:00................................	10:00................................	10:00................................
11:00................................	11:00................................	11:00................................	11:00................................
12:00................................	12:00................................	12:00................................	12:00................................
1:00..................................	1:00..................................	1:00..................................	1:00..................................
2:00..................................	2:00..................................	2:00..................................	2:00..................................
3:00..................................	3:00..................................	3:00..................................	3:00..................................
4:00..................................	4:00..................................	4:00..................................	4:00..................................
5:00..................................	5:00..................................	5:00..................................	5:00..................................
6:00..................................	6:00..................................	6:00..................................	6:00..................................
7:00..................................	7:00..................................	7:00..................................	7:00..................................
8:00..................................	8:00..................................	8:00..................................	8:00..................................
9:00..................................	9:00..................................	9:00..................................	9:00..................................
10:00................................	10:00................................	10:00................................	10:00................................
11:00................................	11:00................................	11:00................................	11:00................................
12:00................................	12:00................................	12:00................................	12:00................................

MILESTONES REACHED

REFLECTION ON LAST WEEK

BIGGEST WINS OF LAST WEEK	THINGS TO BE GRATEFUL FOR
IDENTIFY TIME WASTERS	...AND HOW TO REDUCE AND ELIMINATE THEM
SELF-IMPROVEMENT IDEAS	GOALS FOR THE WEEK AHEAD

REWARD FOR HITTING GOALS

What worked?

What didn't work?

What needs improving?

What are my next actions?

WEEK: _____	MONDAY	TUESDAY	WEDNESDAY
Goal	Goal	Goal	Goal
SECUNDARY TASKS	Priorities	Priorities	Priorities

SECUNDARY TASKS	Priorities	Priorities	Priorities
	1...	1...	1...
	2...	2...	2...
	3...	3...	.
	.		3...
	6:00...	6:0	6:00...
	7:00...	7:0	7:00...
	8:00...	8:0	8:00...
	9:00...	9:0	9:00...
	10:00.......................................	10:0	10:00.......................................
ADITIONAL TASKS	11:00.......................................	11:0	11:00.......................................
	12:00.......................................	12:0	12:00.......................................
	1:00...	1:00...	1:00...
	2:00...	2:00...	2:00...
	.3:00..	3:00...	3:00...
	4:00...	4:00...	4:00...
	5:00...	5:00...	5:00...
	6:00...	6:00...	6:00...
	7:00...	7:00...	7:00...
	8:00...	8:00...	8:00...
	9:00...	9:00...	9:00...
	10:00.......................................	10:00.......................................	10:00.......................................
	11:00.......................................	11:00.......................................	11:00.......................................
	12:00.......................................	12:00.......................................	12:00.......................................

HABIT TRACKER			M	T	W	T	F	S	S

THURSDAY	FRIDAY	SATURDAY	SUNDAY
Goal	Goal	Goal	Goal
Priorities	Priorities	Priorities	Priorities
1.........................	1.........................	1.........................	1.........................
2.........................	2.........................	2.........................	2.........................
.	.	.	.
3.........................	3.........................	3.........................	3.........................
6:00.........................	6:00.........................	6:00.........................	6:00.........................
7:00.........................	7:00.........................	7:00.........................	7:00.........................
8:00.........................	8:00.........................	8:00.........................	8:00.........................
9:00.........................	9:00.........................	9:00.........................	9:00.........................
10:00.........................	10:00.........................	10:00.........................	10:00.........................
11:00.........................	11:00.........................	11:00.........................	11:00.........................
12:00.........................	12:00.........................	12:00.........................	12:00.........................
1:00.........................	1:00.........................	1:00.........................	1:00.........................
2:00.........................	2:00.........................	2:00.........................	2:00.........................
3:00.........................	3:00.........................	3:00.........................	3:00.........................
4:00.........................	4:00.........................	4:00.........................	4:00.........................
5:00.........................	5:00.........................	5:00.........................	5:00.........................
6:00.........................	6:00.........................	6:00.........................	6:00.........................
7:00.........................	7:00.........................	7:00.........................	7:00.........................
8:00.........................	8:00.........................	8:00.........................	8:00.........................
9:00.........................	9:00.........................	9:00.........................	9:00.........................
10:00.........................	10:00.........................	10:00.........................	10:00.........................
11:00.........................	11:00.........................	11:00.........................	11:00.........................
12:00.........................	12:00.........................	12:00.........................	12:00.........................

MILESTONES REACHED

REFLECTION ON LAST WEEK

BIGGEST WINS OF LAST WEEK	THINGS TO BE GRATEFUL FOR
IDENTIFY TIME WASTERS	...AND HOW TO REDUCE AND ELIMINATE THEM
SELF-IMPROVEMENT IDEAS	GOALS FOR THE WEEK AHEAD

REWARD FOR HITTING GOALS

What worked?

What didn't work?

What needs improving?

What are my next actions?

END OF YEAR REFLECTION

What were the three biggest lessons you've learned this past year?

Review your planner for this past year and assess your priorities. Are you happy with how you spent your time? If not, what steps can you take for the next year to adjust them?

What did you accomplish this past year? What are you most proud of?

Name three things you can improve on next year. What concrete actions can you take to work towards these improvements?

What or who are you especially grateful for this past year?

Review what you wrote on the beginning of this planner about your life's vision. Have you progressed towards your goals? Are you nearer the life you want?

List your goals for next year. Divide them into smaller goals. Think about how you can achieve them. What are your next steps?

NOTES

NOTES

NOTES

Thank you for getting your blessed hands on this life changing work of creative art. I'd love to read all about your unique transformation. Share your best Review:

https://www.amazon.com/author/jacquelinensamuels

While there, check out the other books I've created for your personal and family's empowerment and enjoyment.

For more awesome resources visit:

https://serveandthrive.gumroad.com

Video courses:

https://serve-and-thrive-academy.thinkific.com/

To your blessed lifestyle and purpose,

Dr Jackie Samuels

*Author, Songwriter, Speaker, Educator, Winner of 1ˢᵗ ever **Best Female Actress Trophy** at the **Kisima Awards Show** in Nairobi, Kenya (1997)*

SERVE & THRIVE

ACADEMY

Thank you for purchasing this Productivity resource.

For more info visit us at:
Training: https://serve-and-thrive-academy.thinkific.com/
Shop Resources: https://serveandthrive.gumroad.com/
Amazon Books: https://tinyurl.com/AuthorJNSamuelsUK
Kindly leave us your best Review on Amazon. Look forward to serving you again.

Dr Jackie Samuels

Printed in Great Britain
by Amazon

21161973R00133